PICTURES FROM THE EDGE

PHIL JONES

www.1889books.co.uk

ISBN: 978-1-915045-41-6

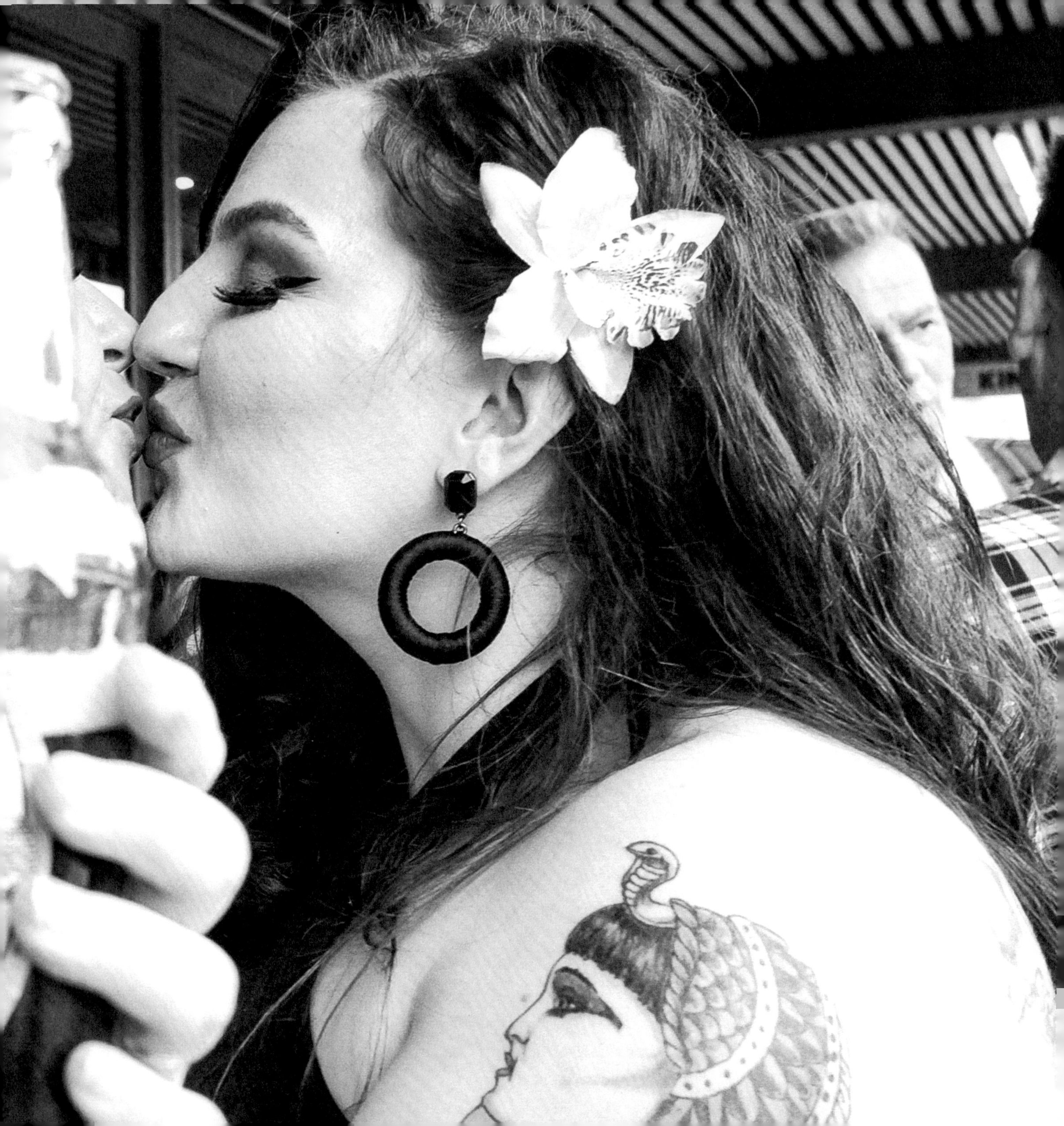

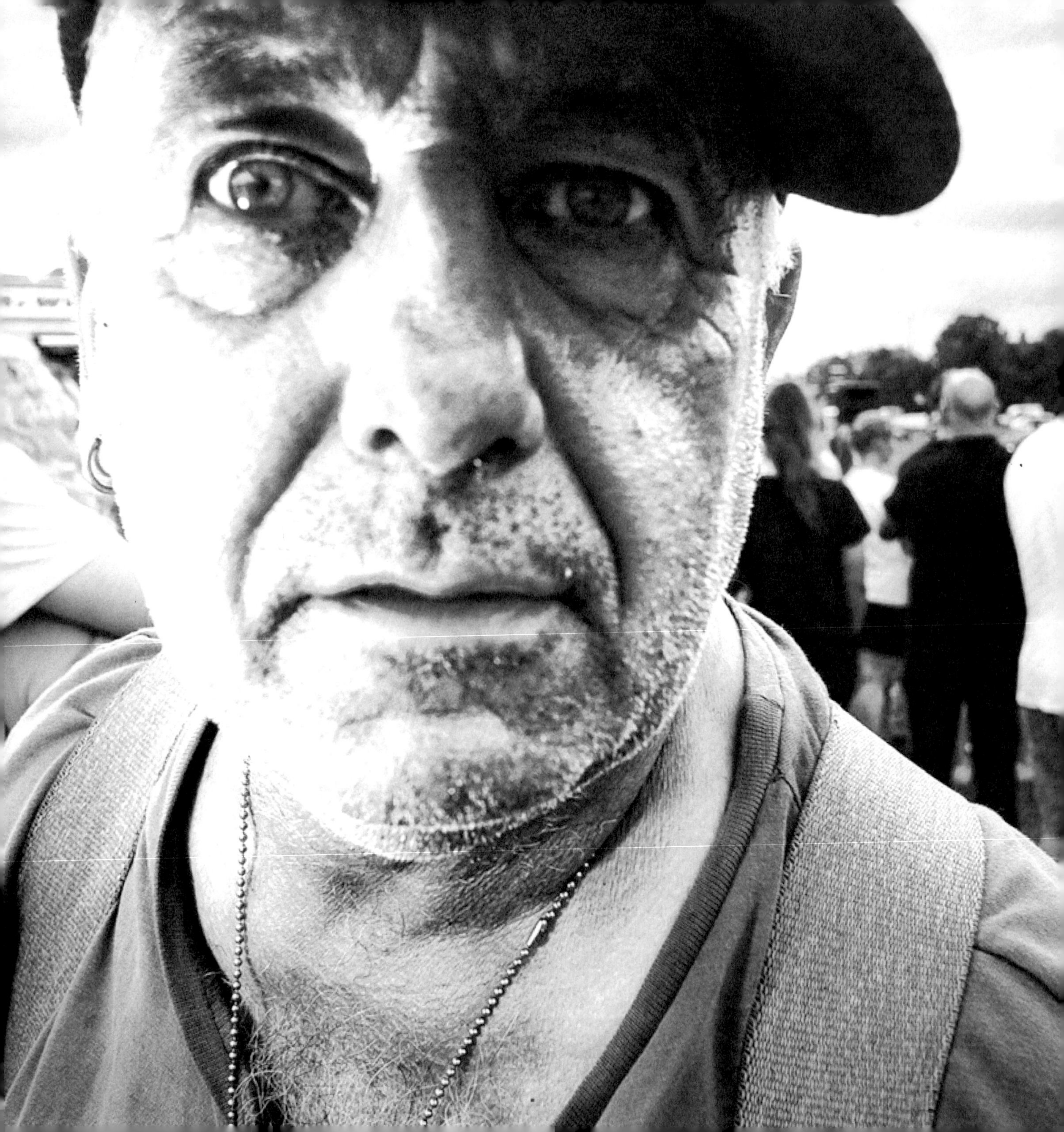

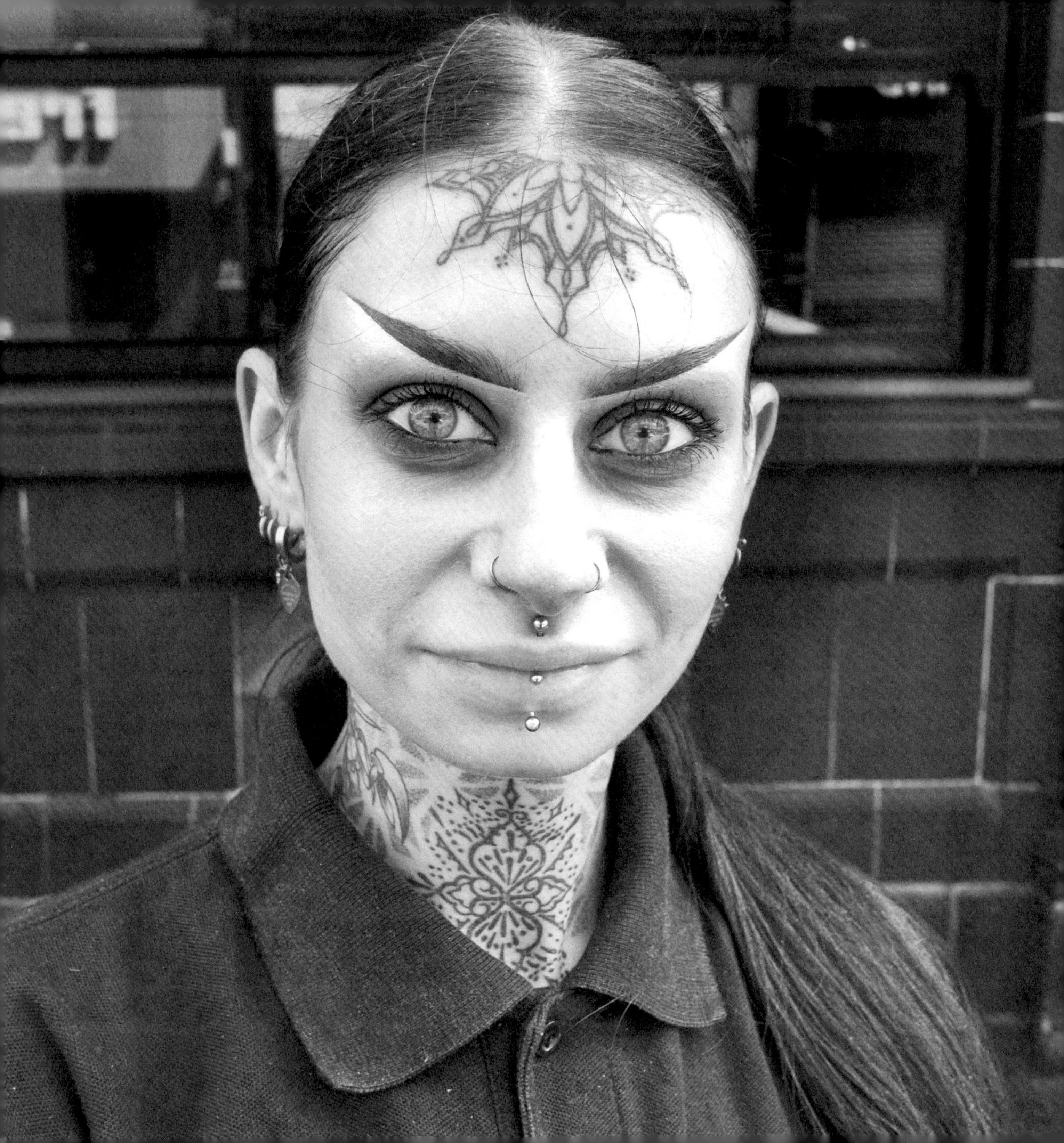

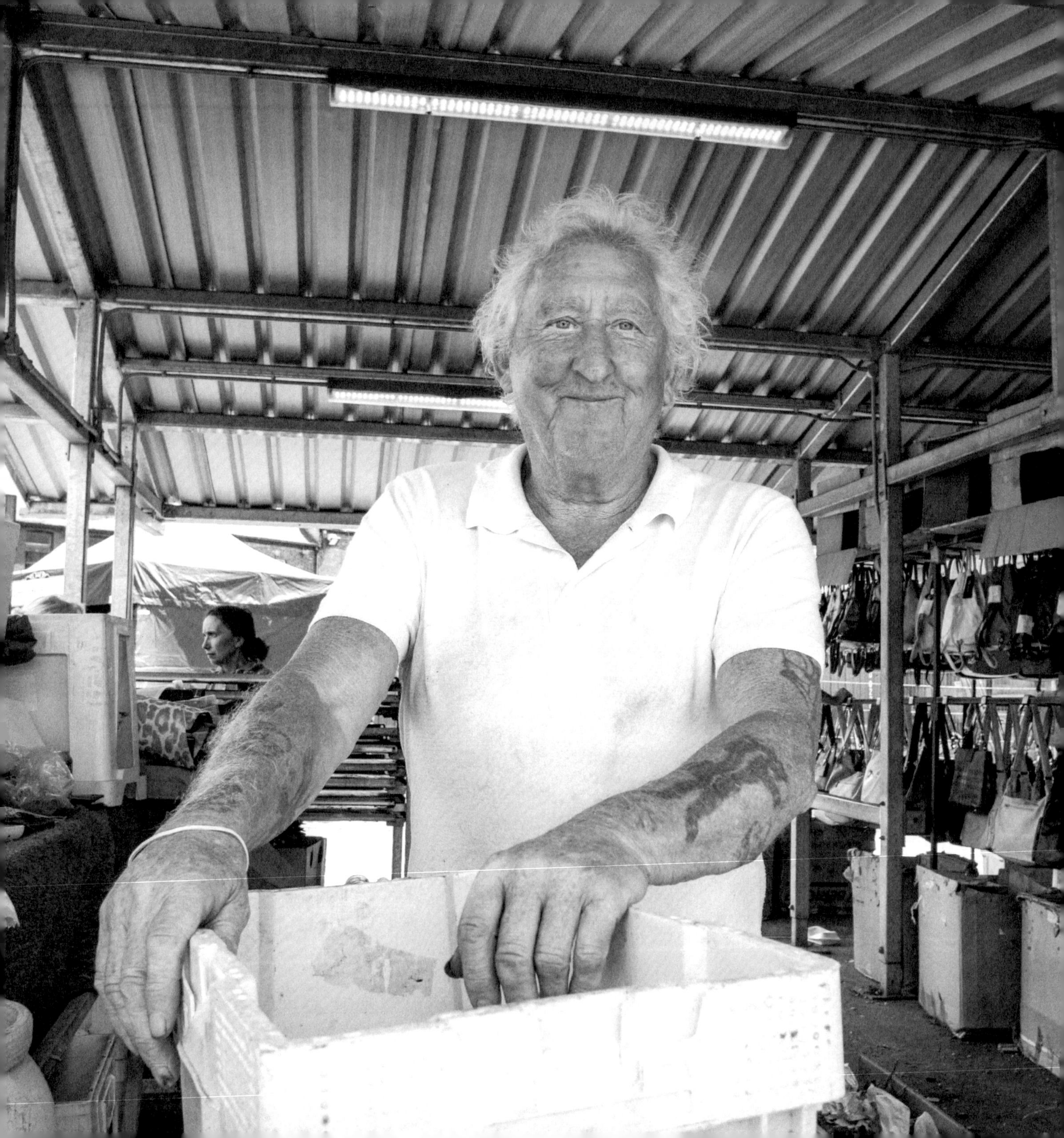

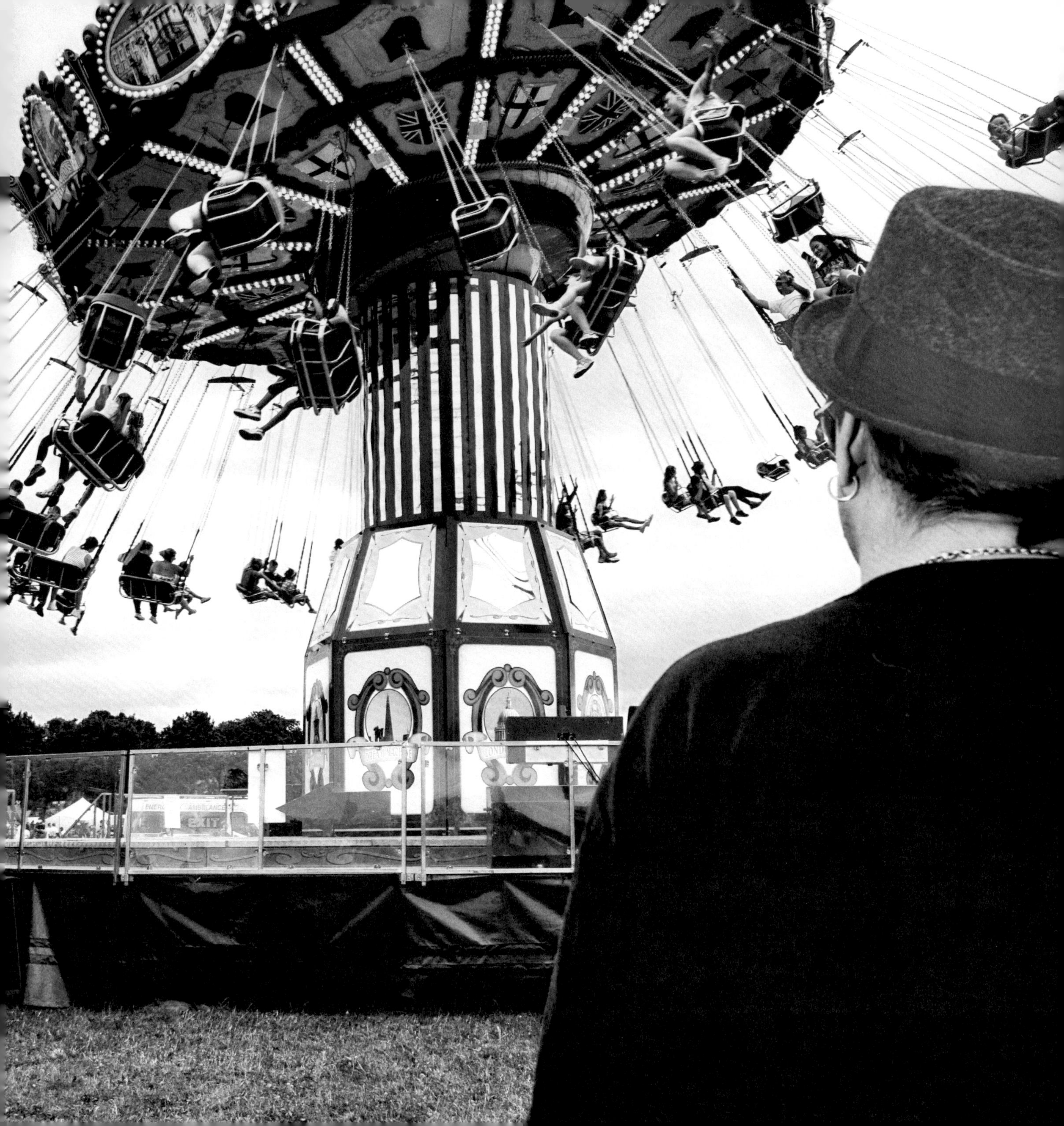

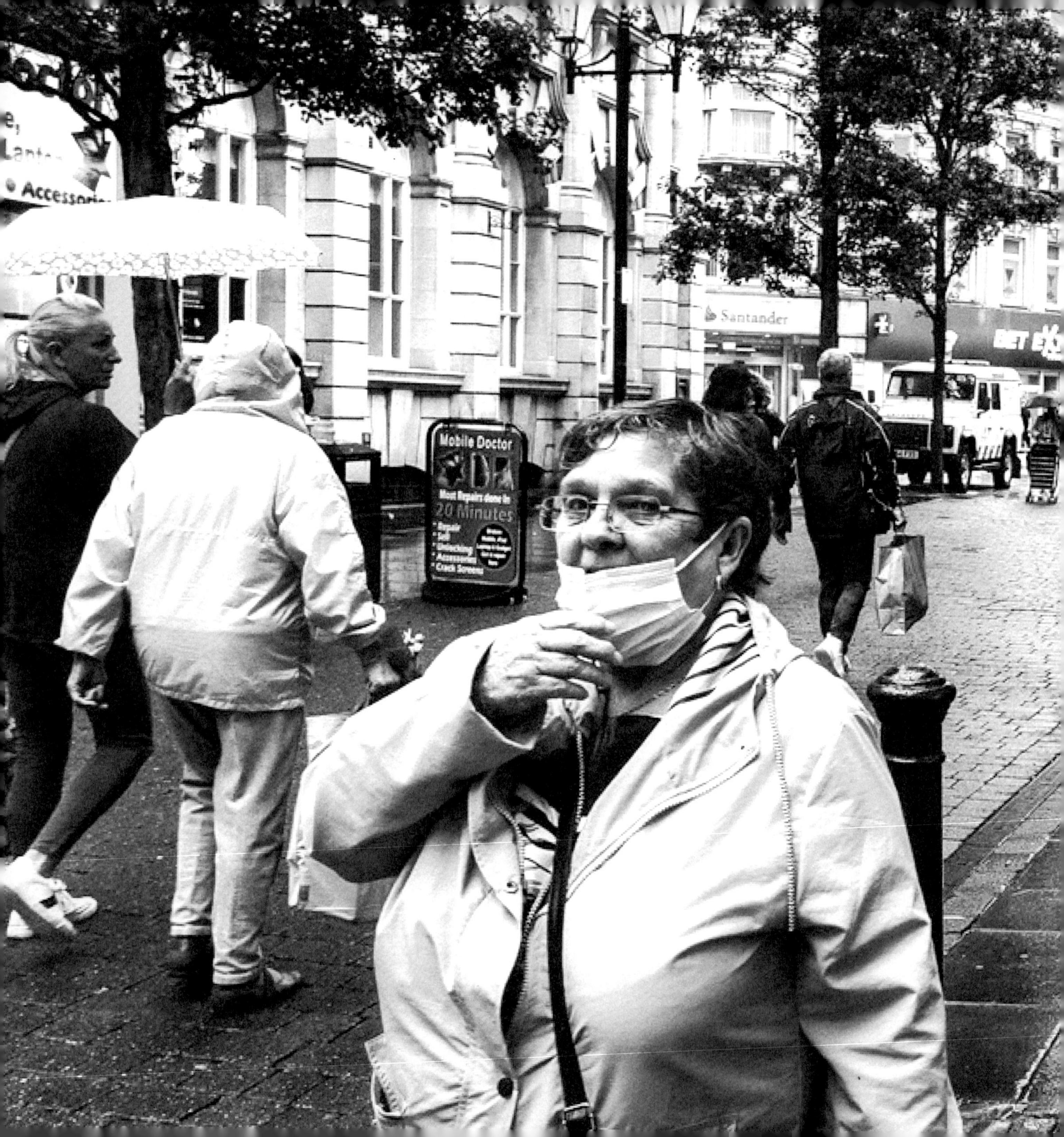
Accessori
Mobile Doctor
Most Repairs done in
20 Minutes
Santander
BET

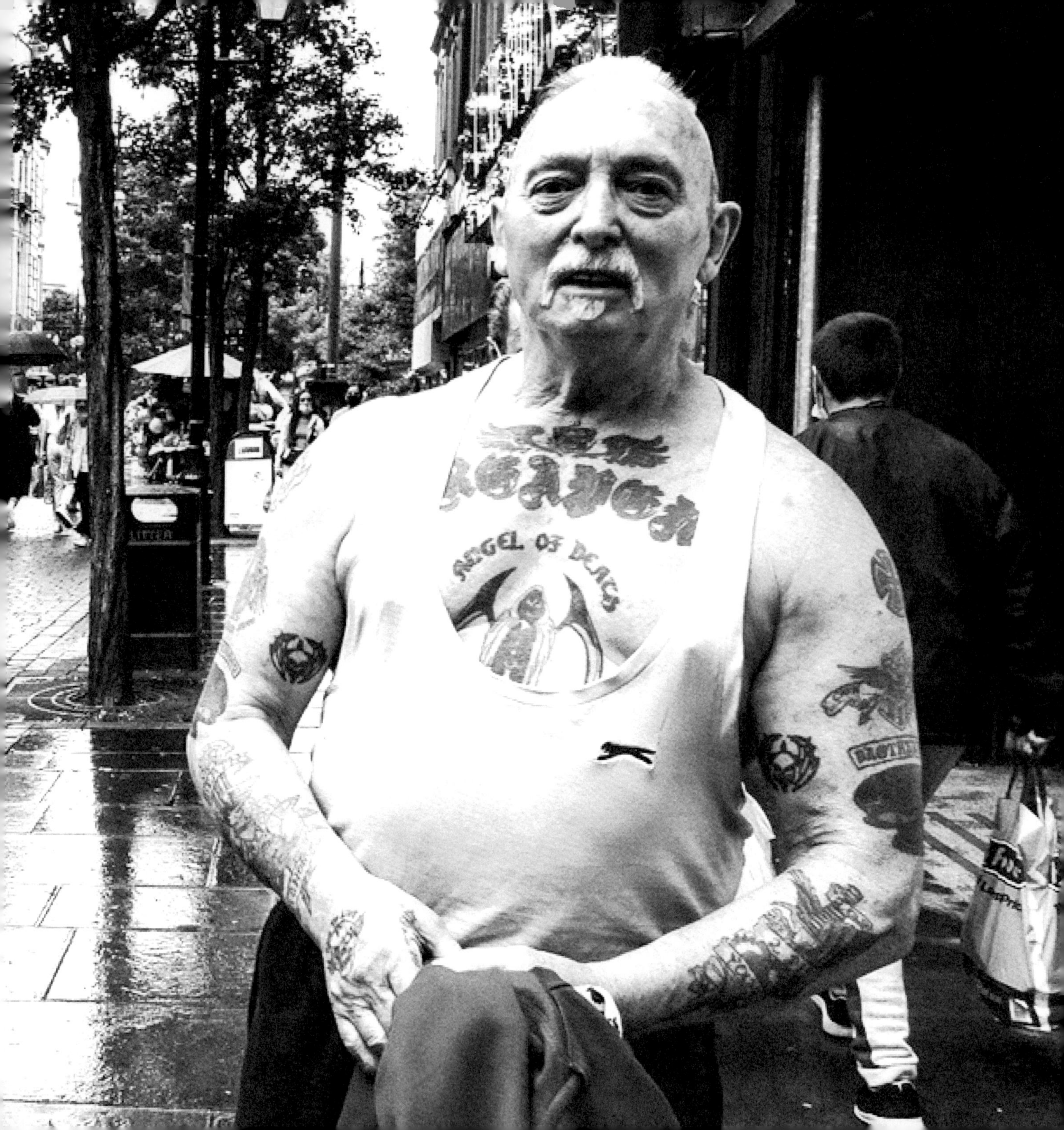

ANGEL OF DEATH

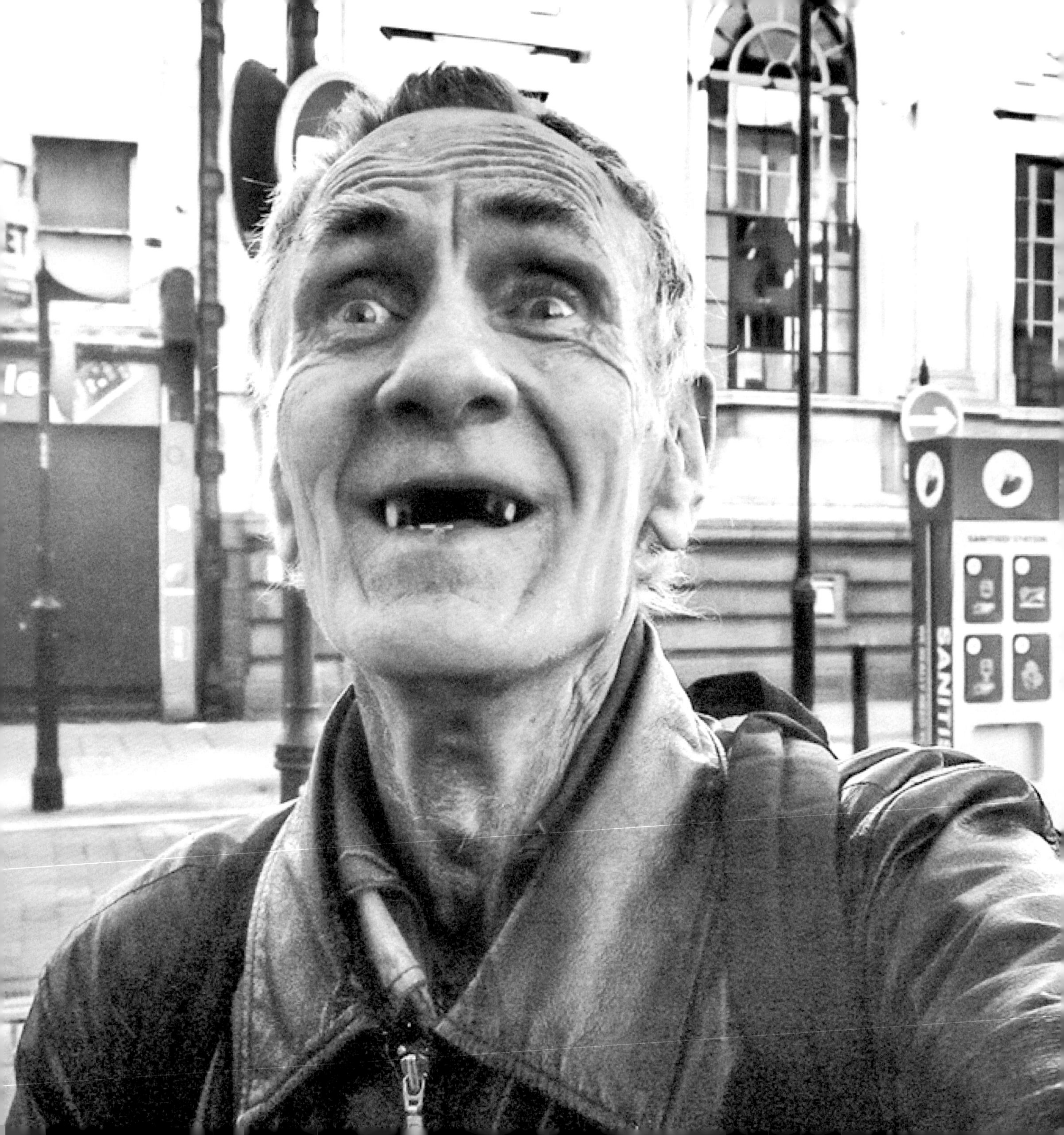

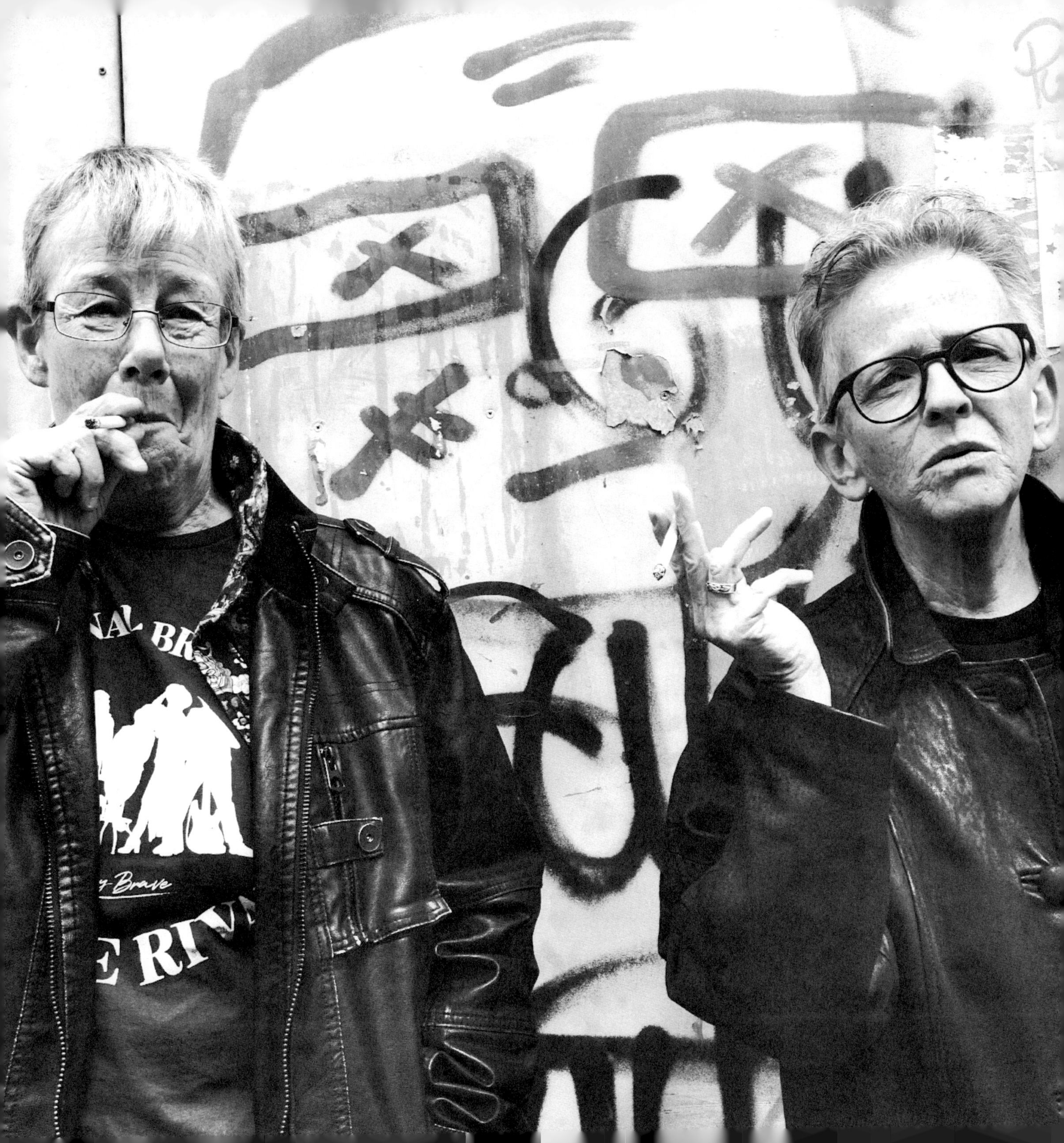

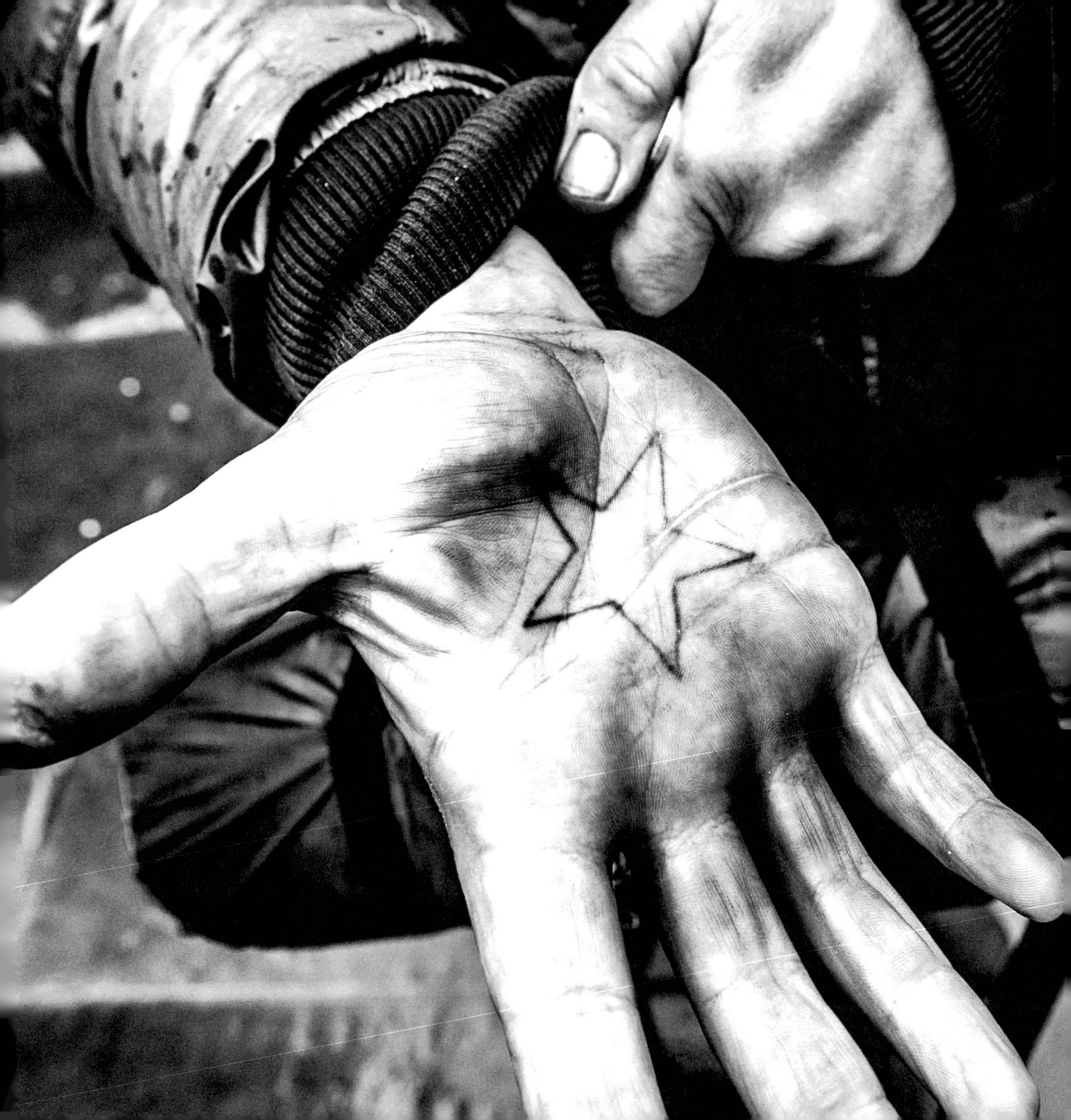

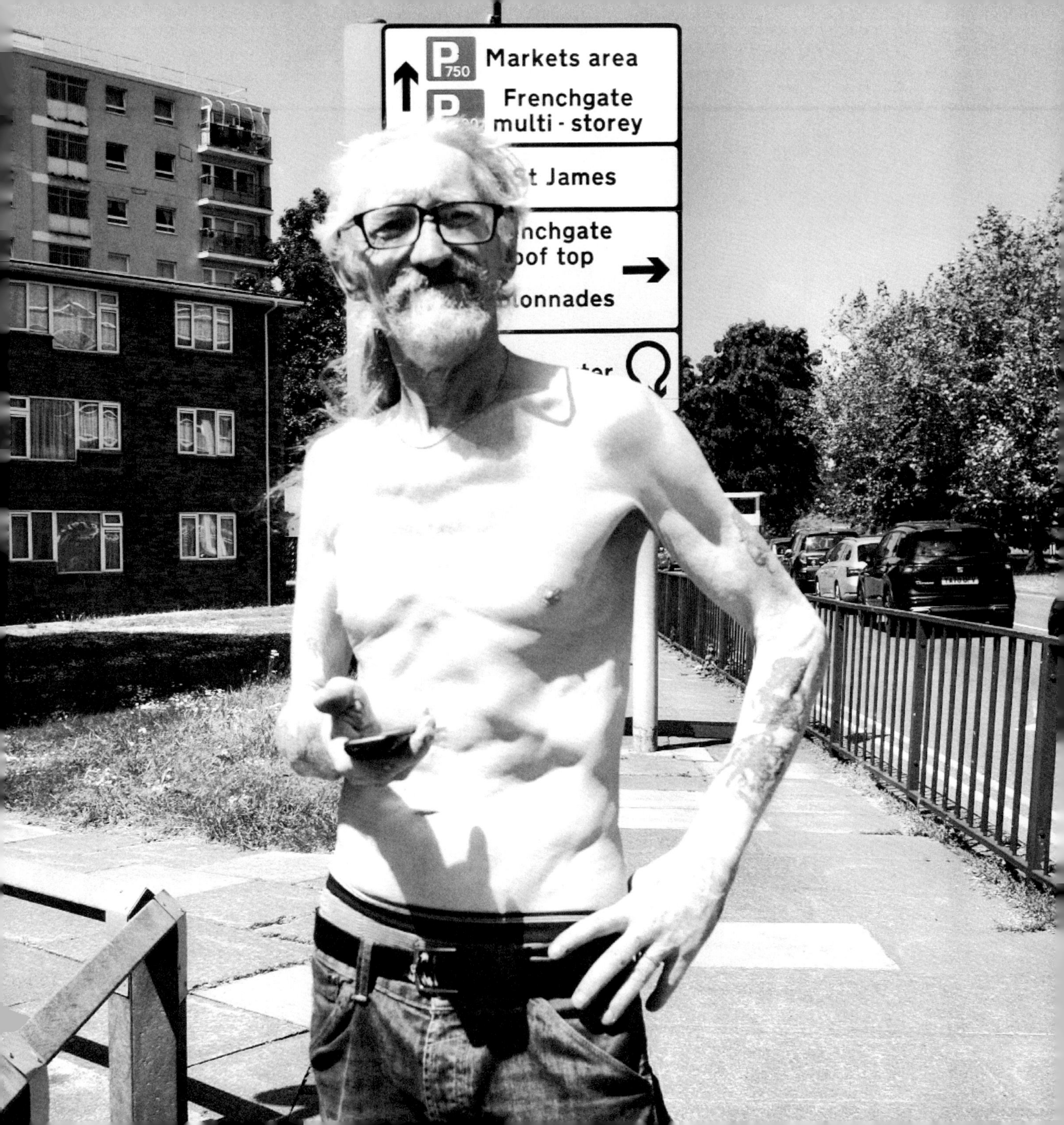

P 750 Markets area
P Frenchgate multi - storey
St James
nchgate of top
tonnades
ter

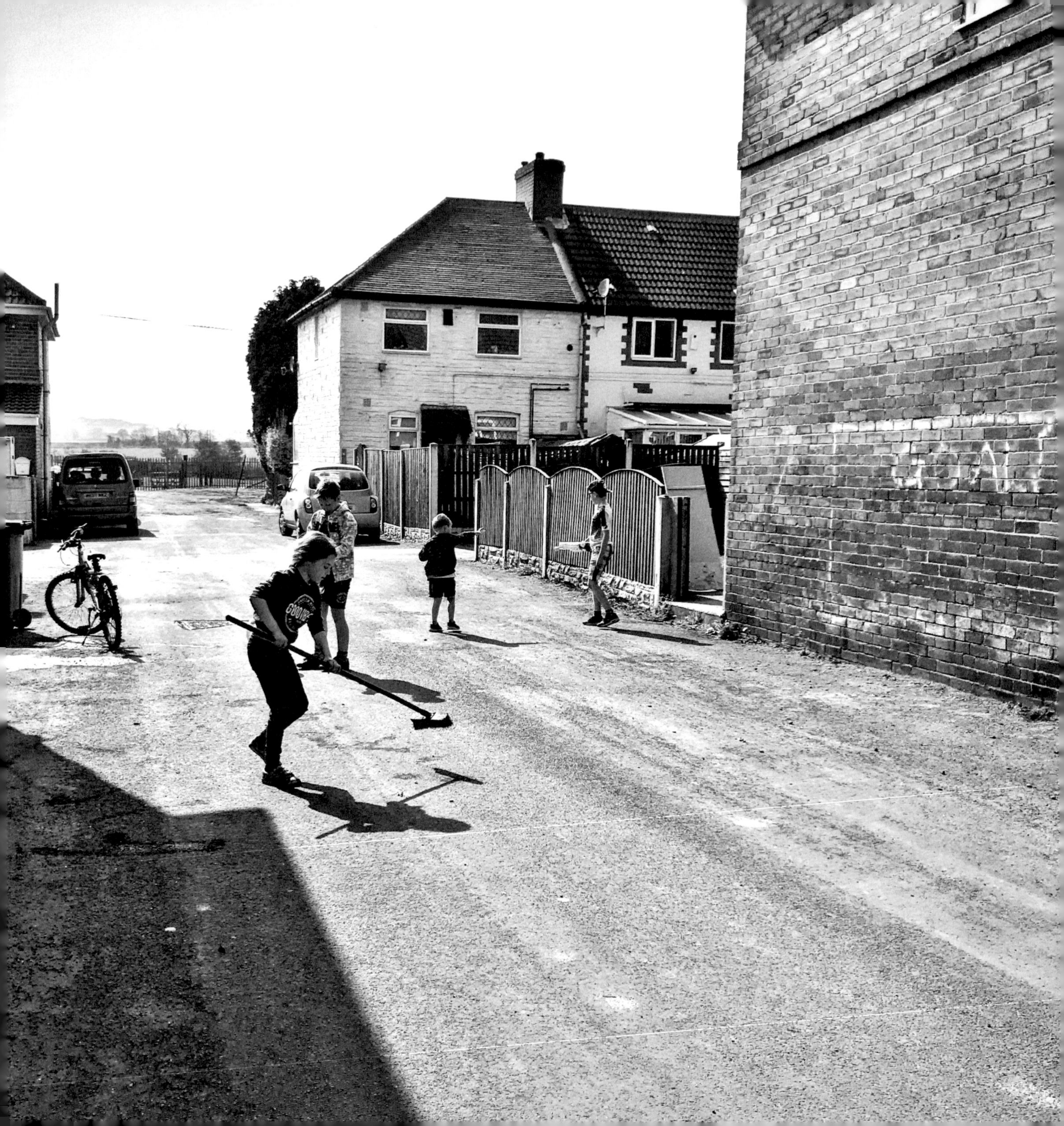

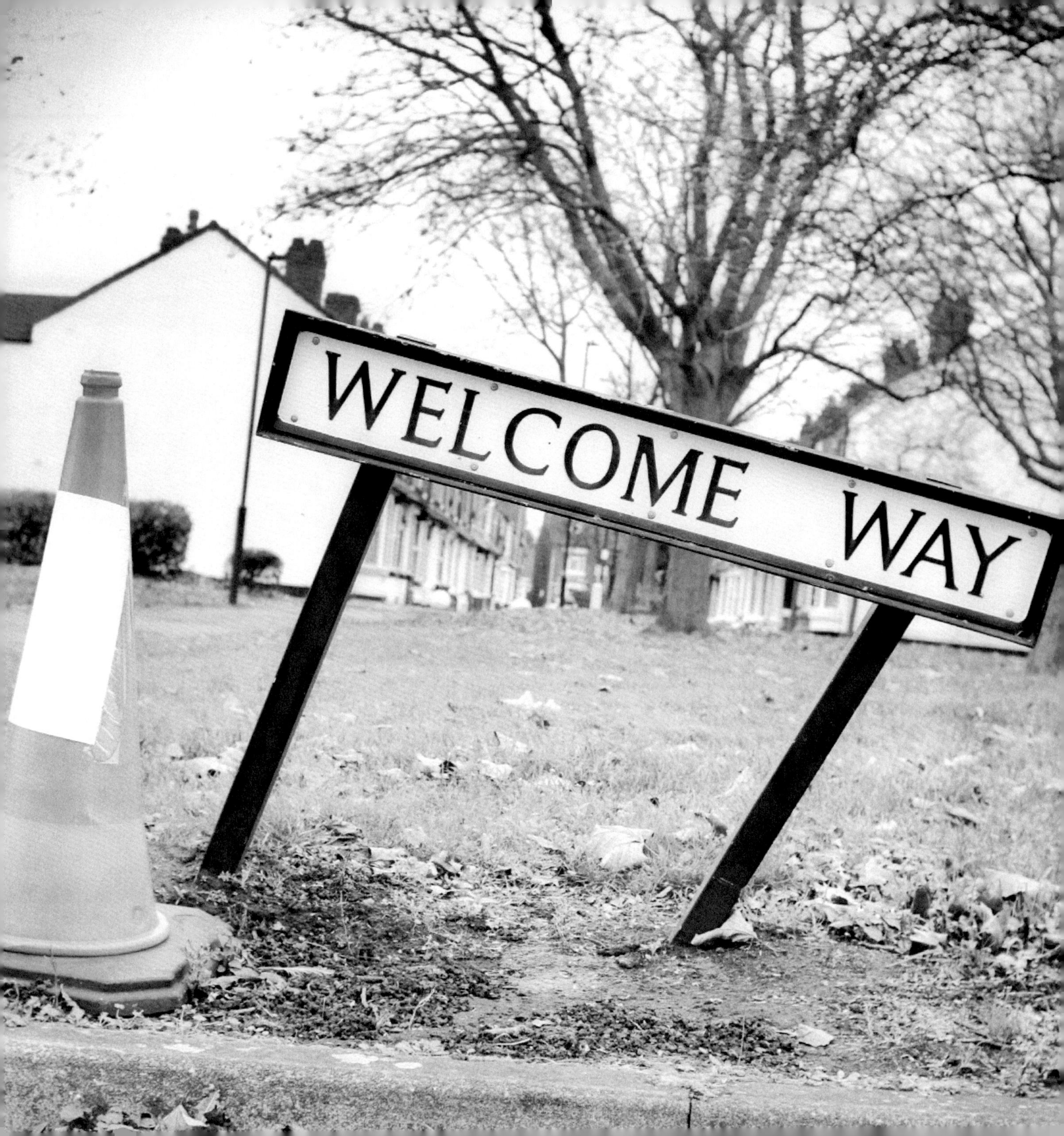

WELCOME WAY

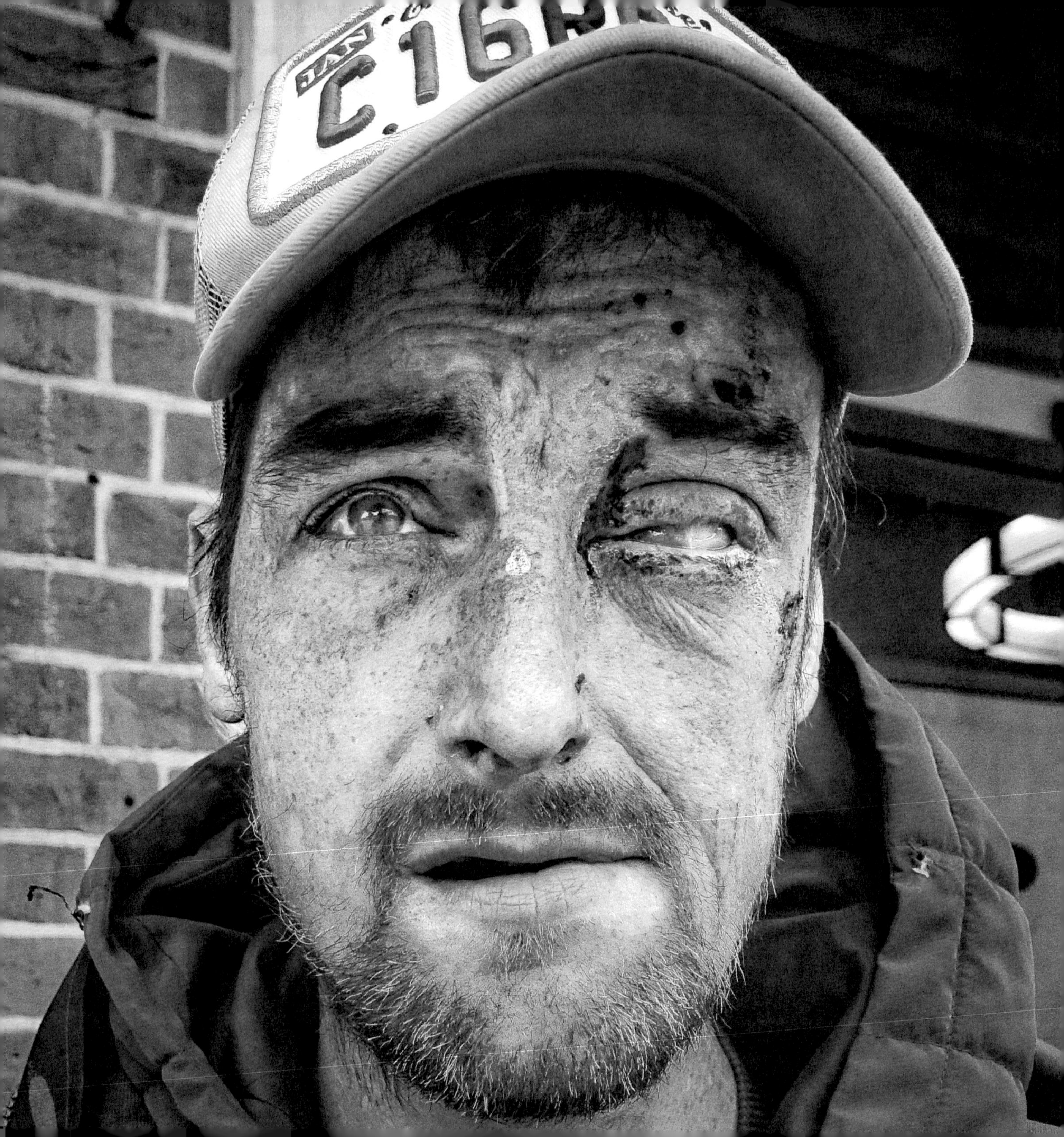

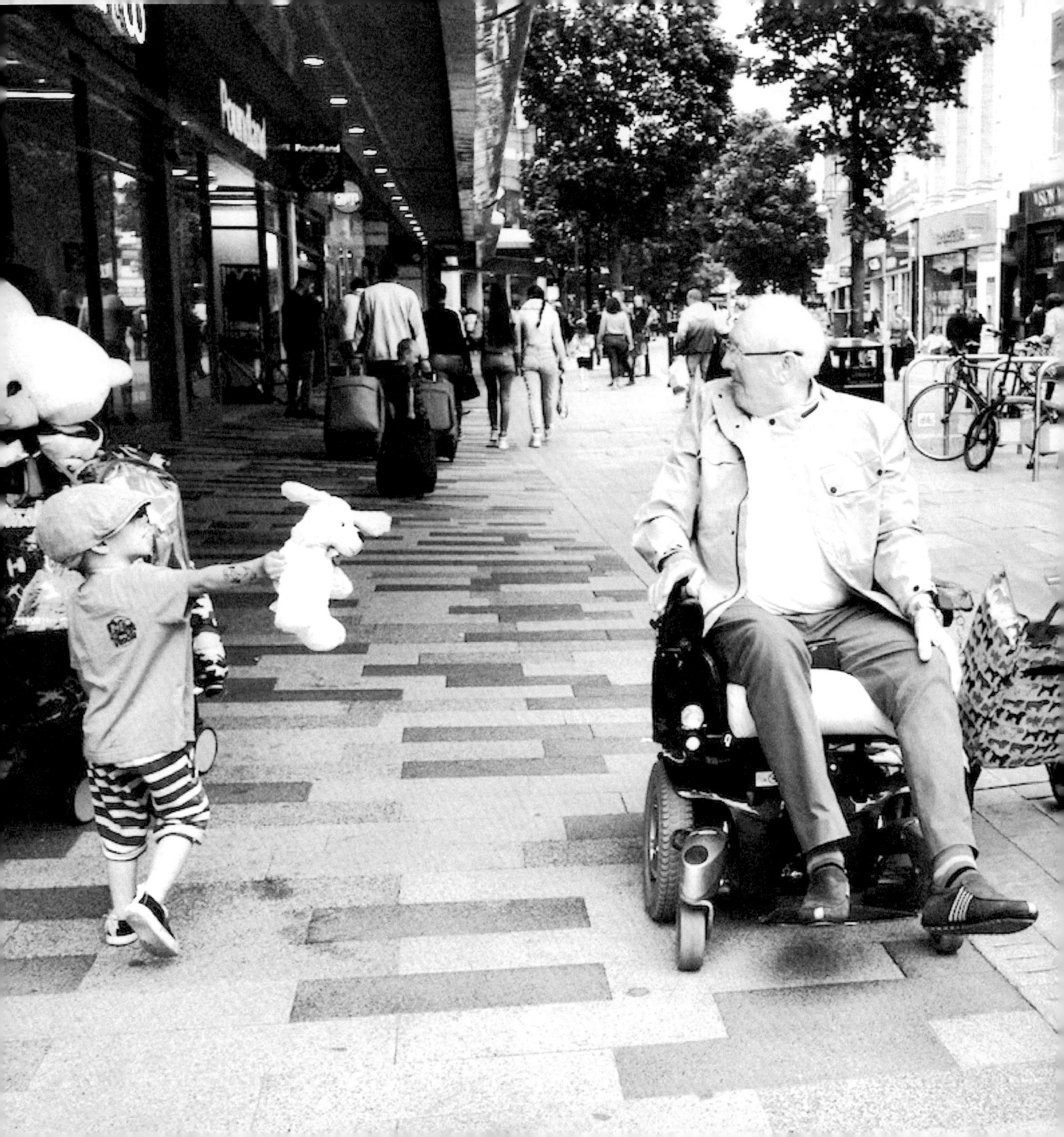

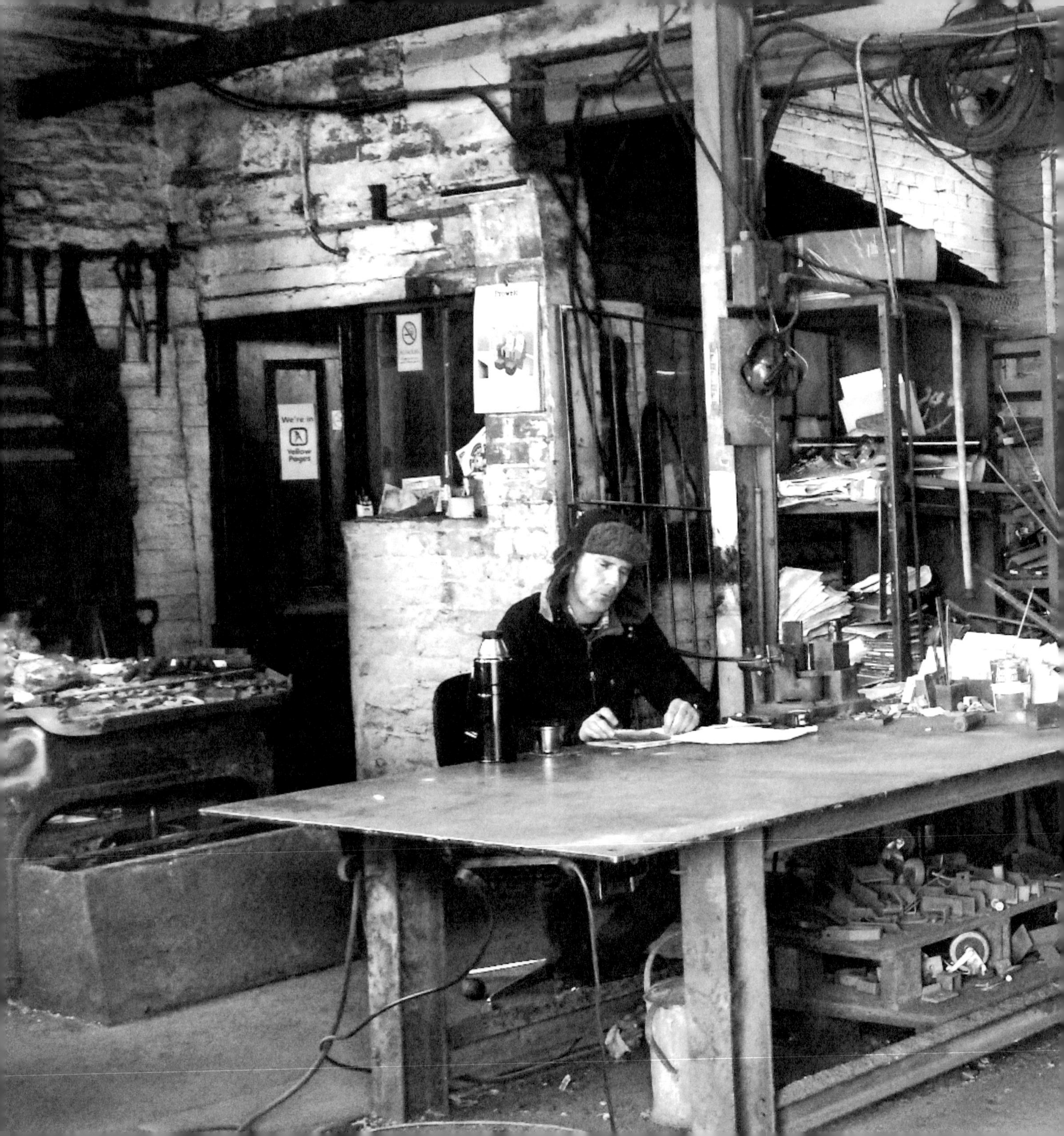

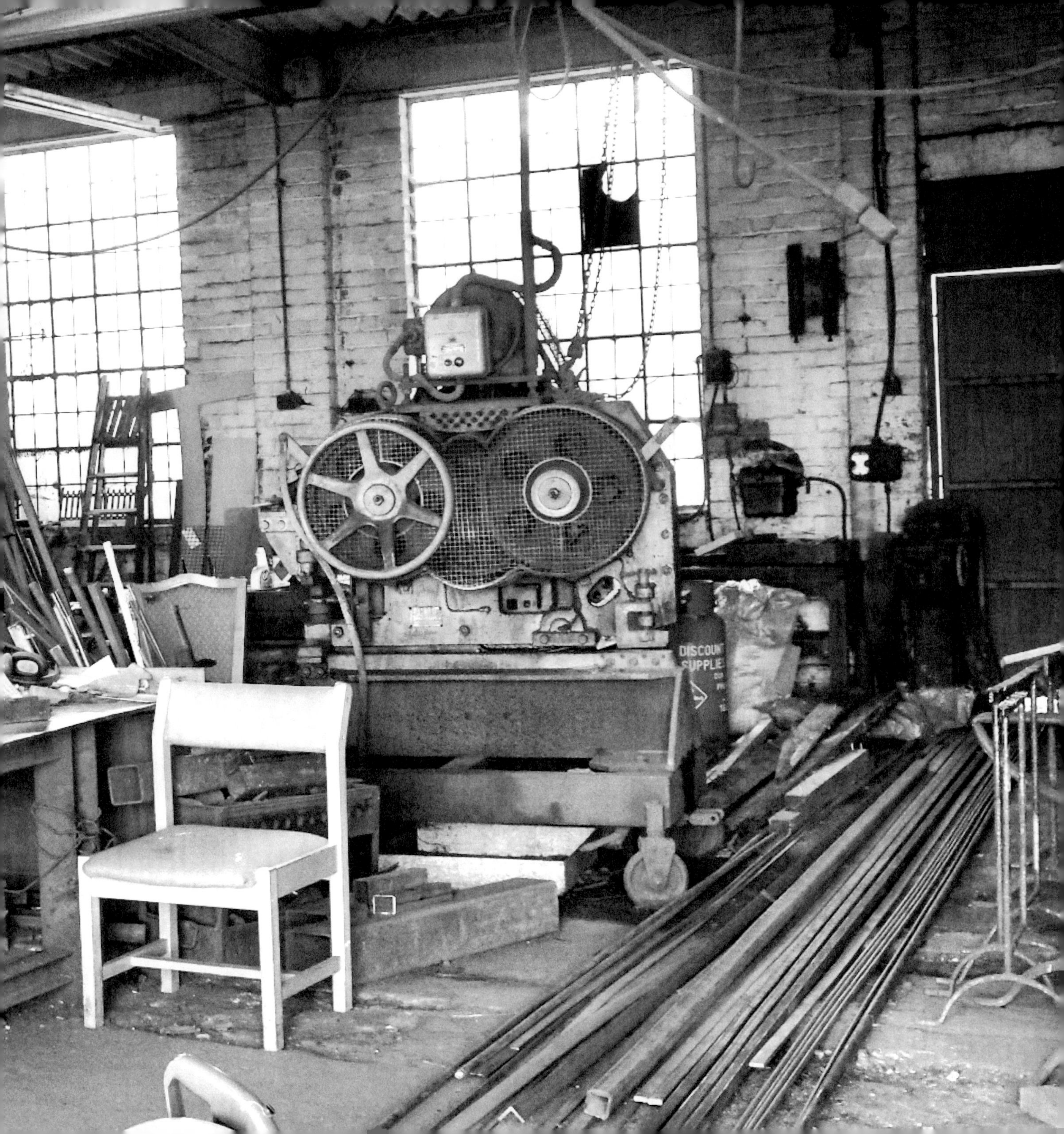

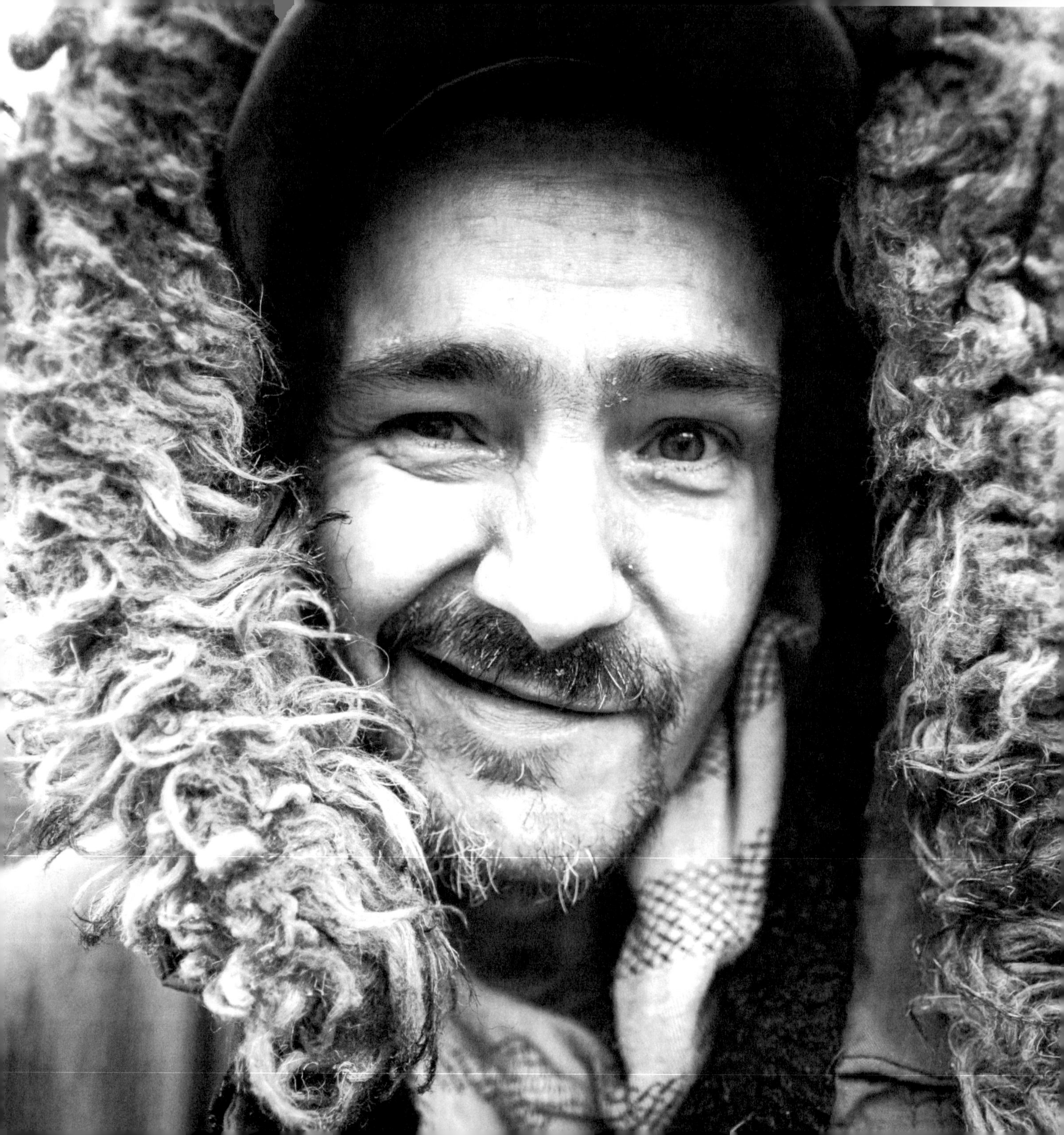

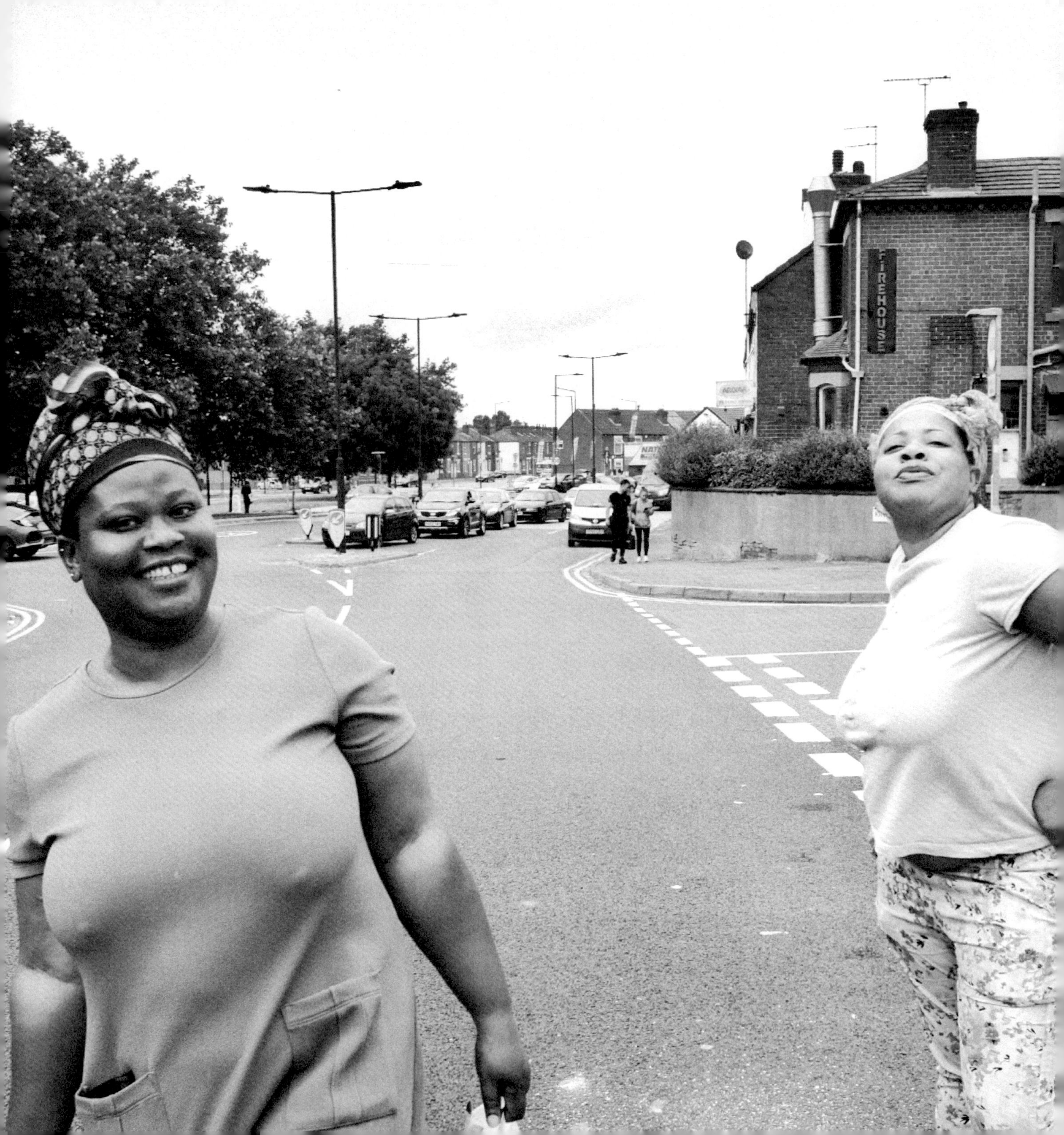
FIREHOUSE

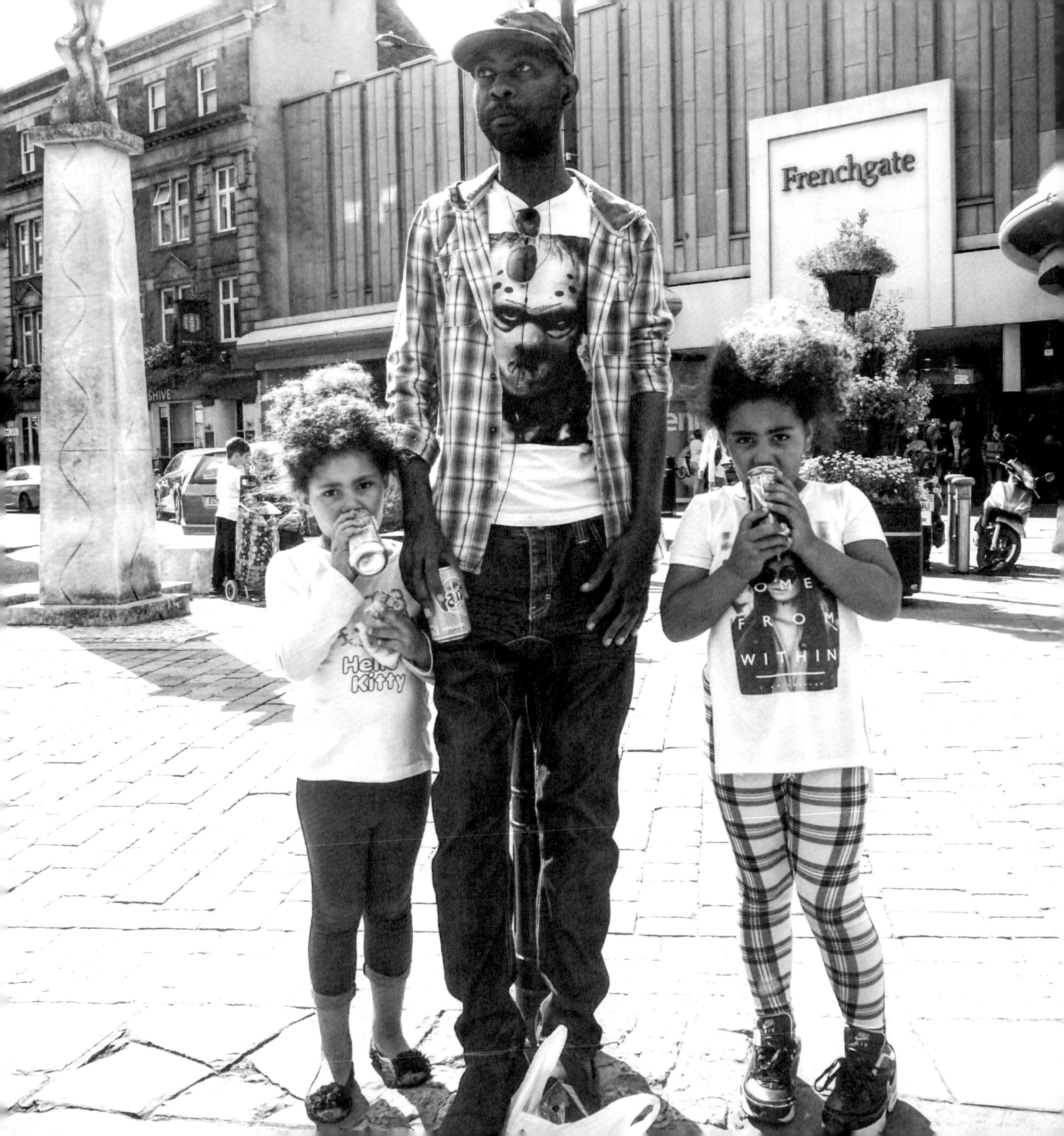
Frenchgate

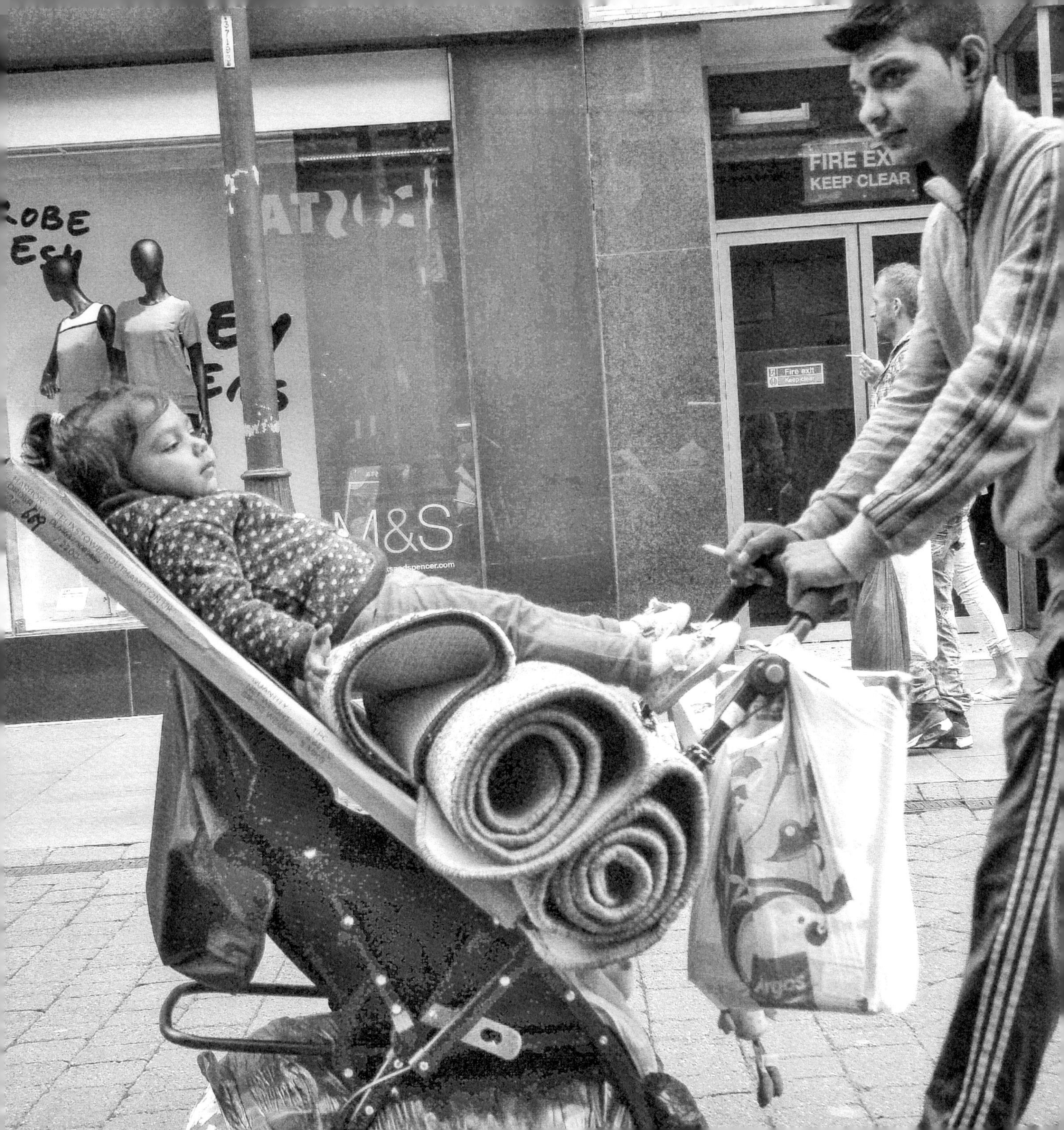
FIRE EXIT
KEEP CLEAR
Fire exit
Keep clear
M&S
marksandspencer.com
Argos

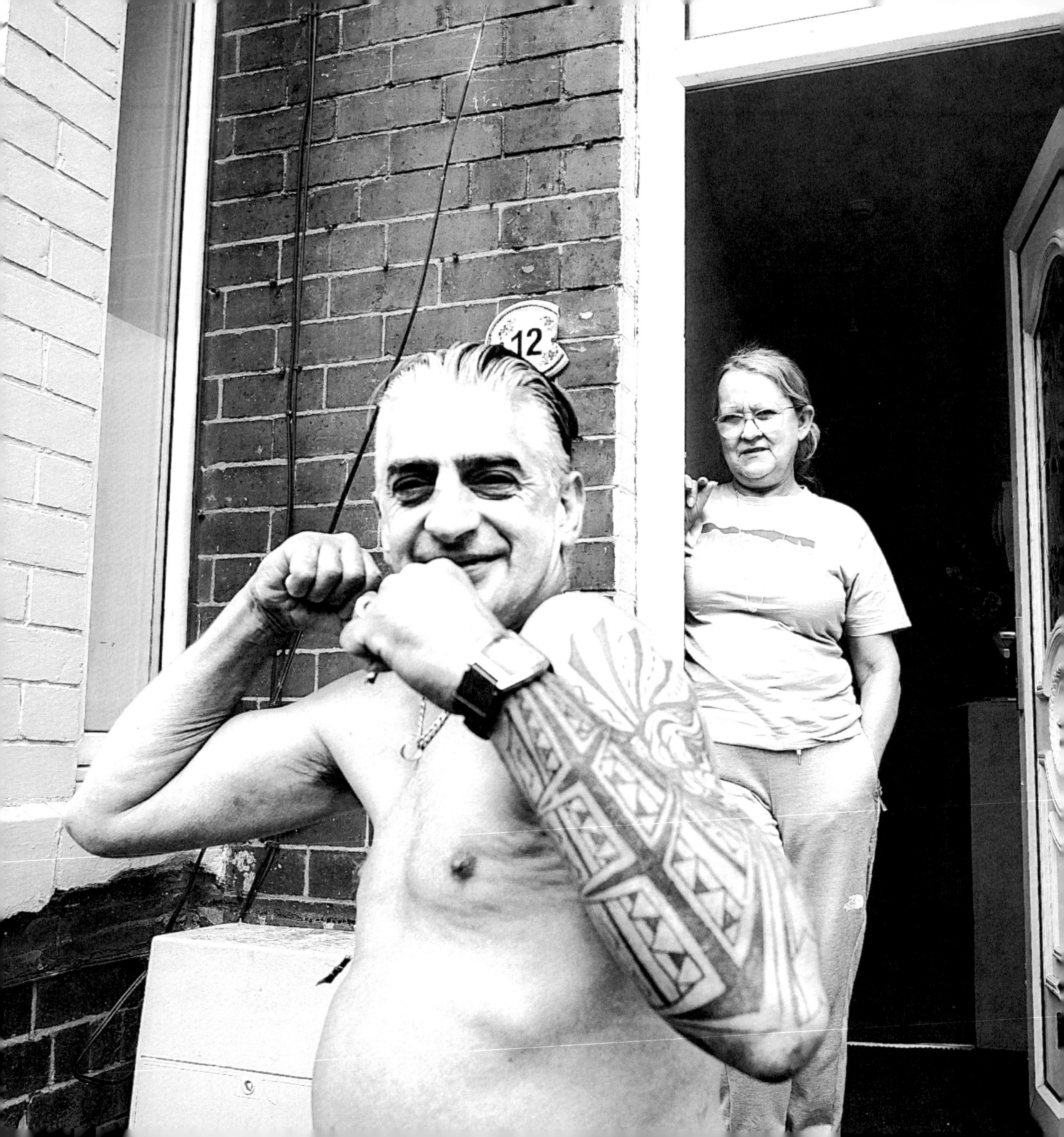

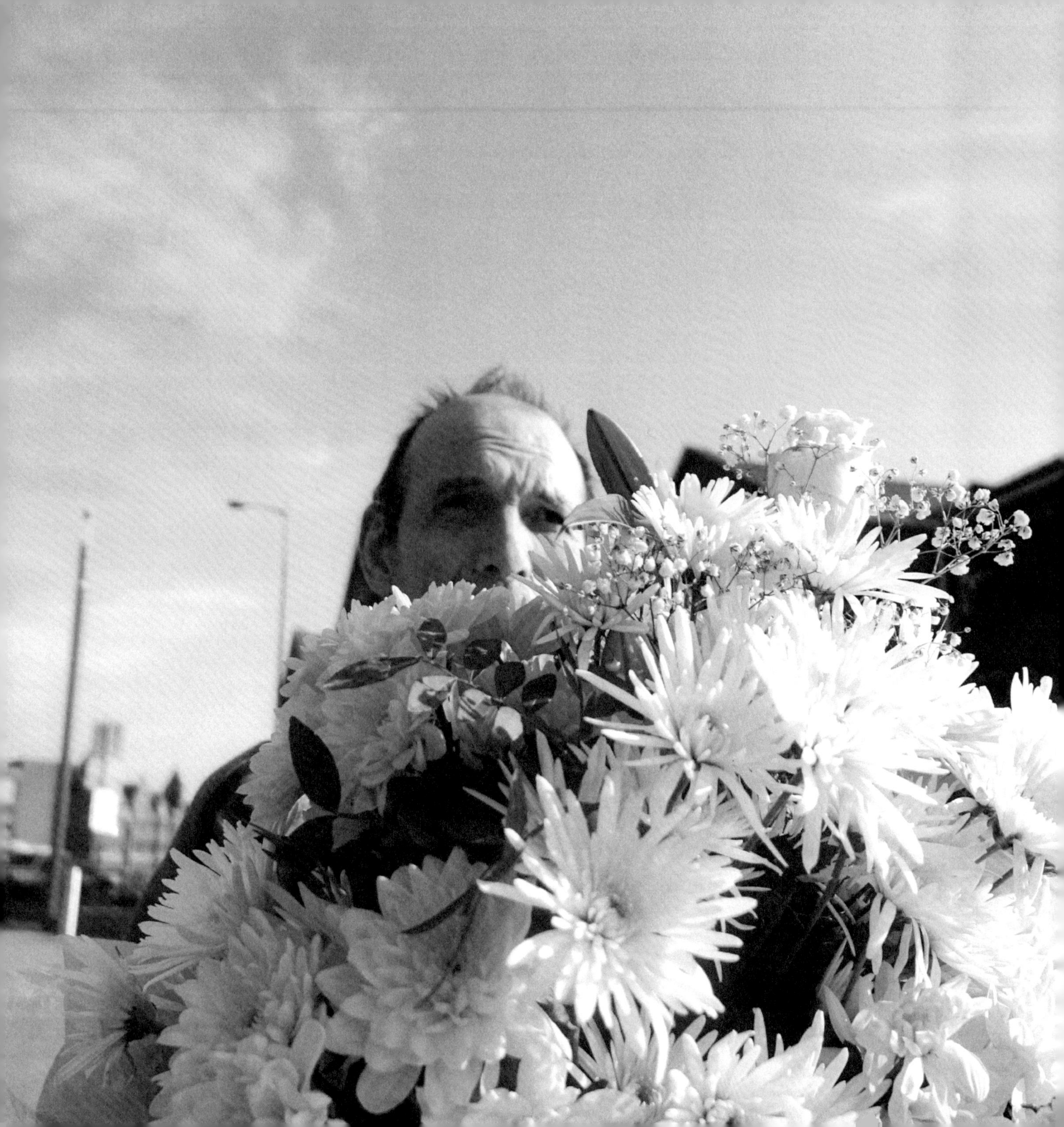

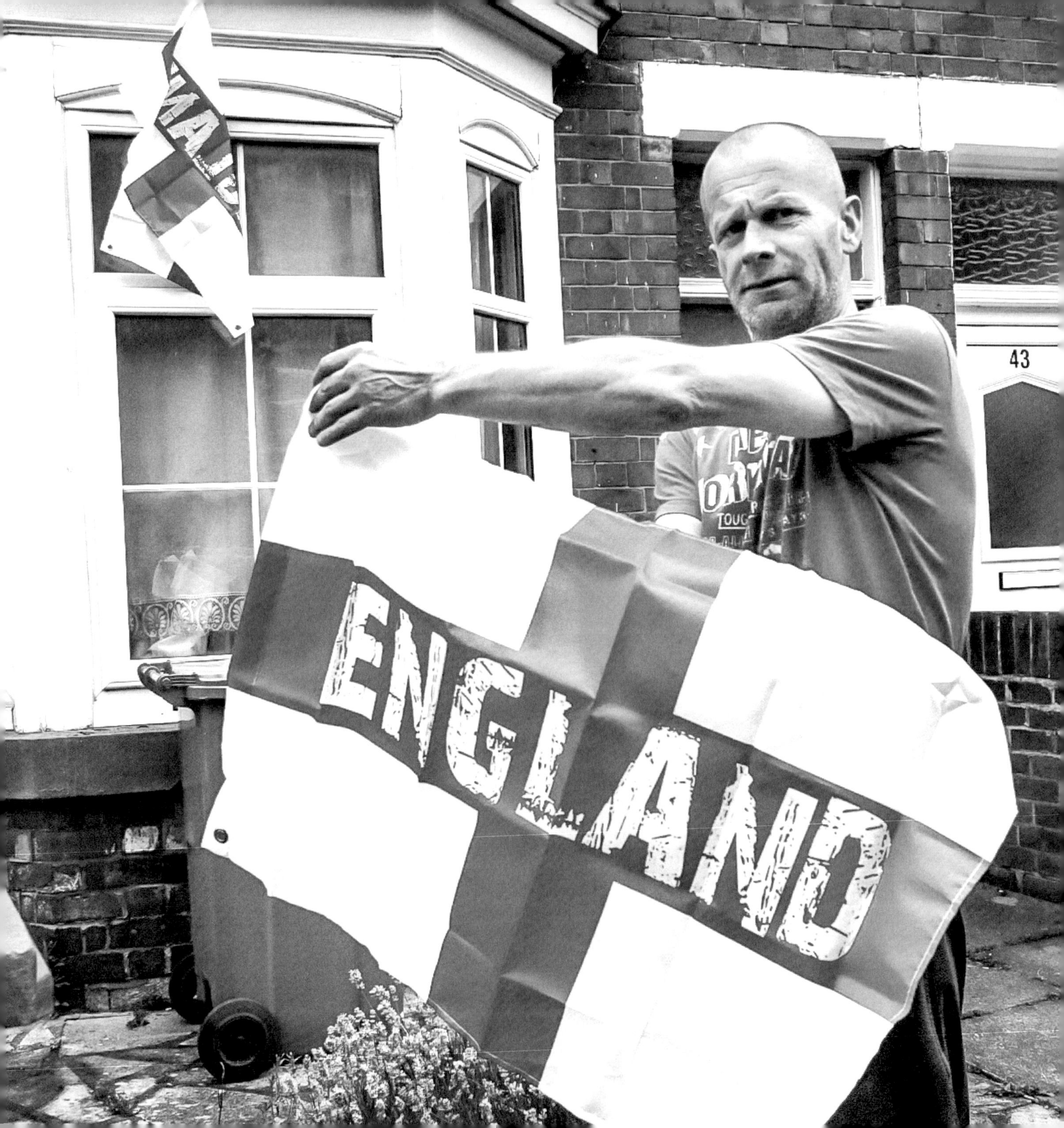

ENGLAND
43

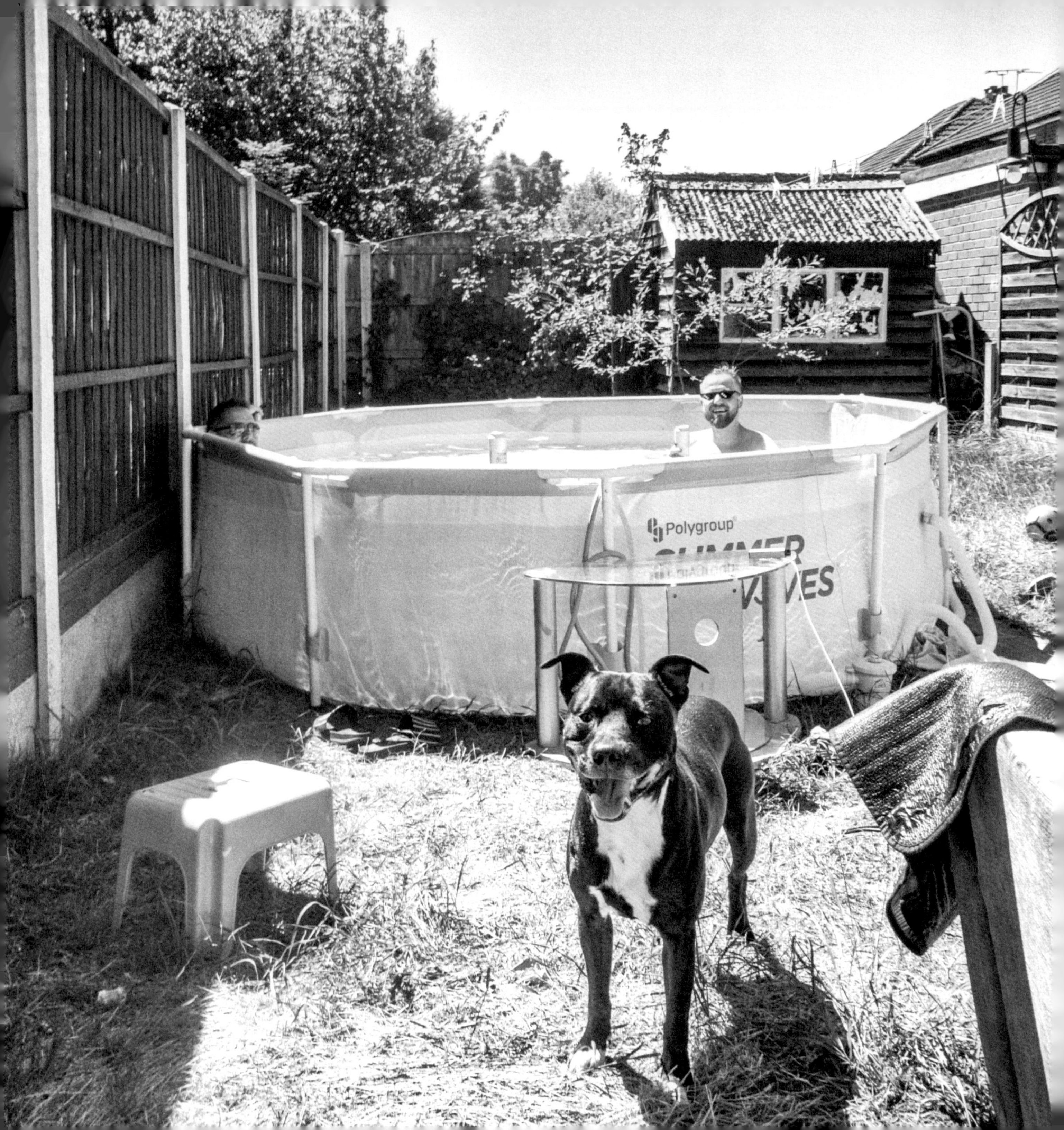

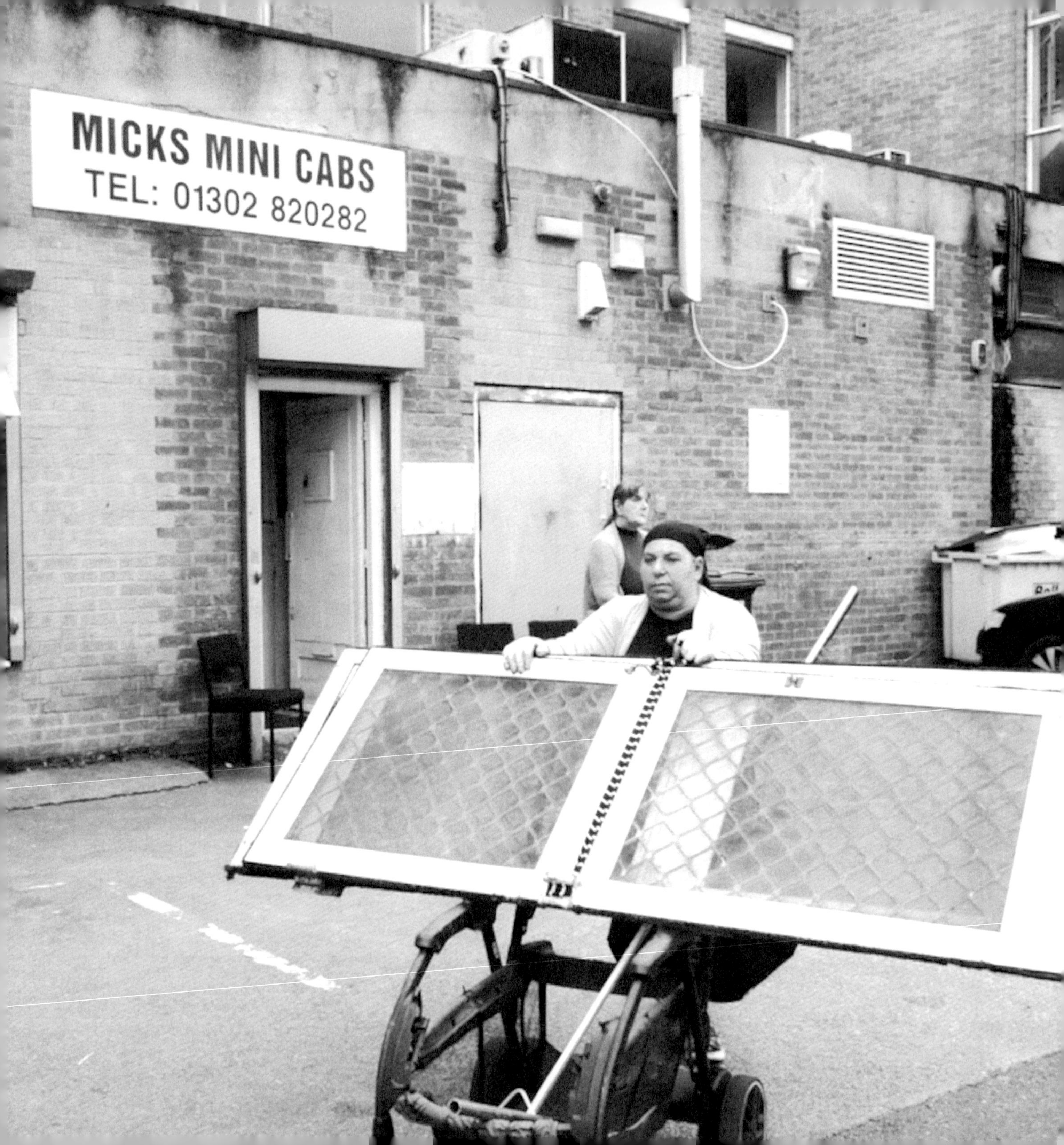

MICKS MINI CABS
TEL: 01302 820282

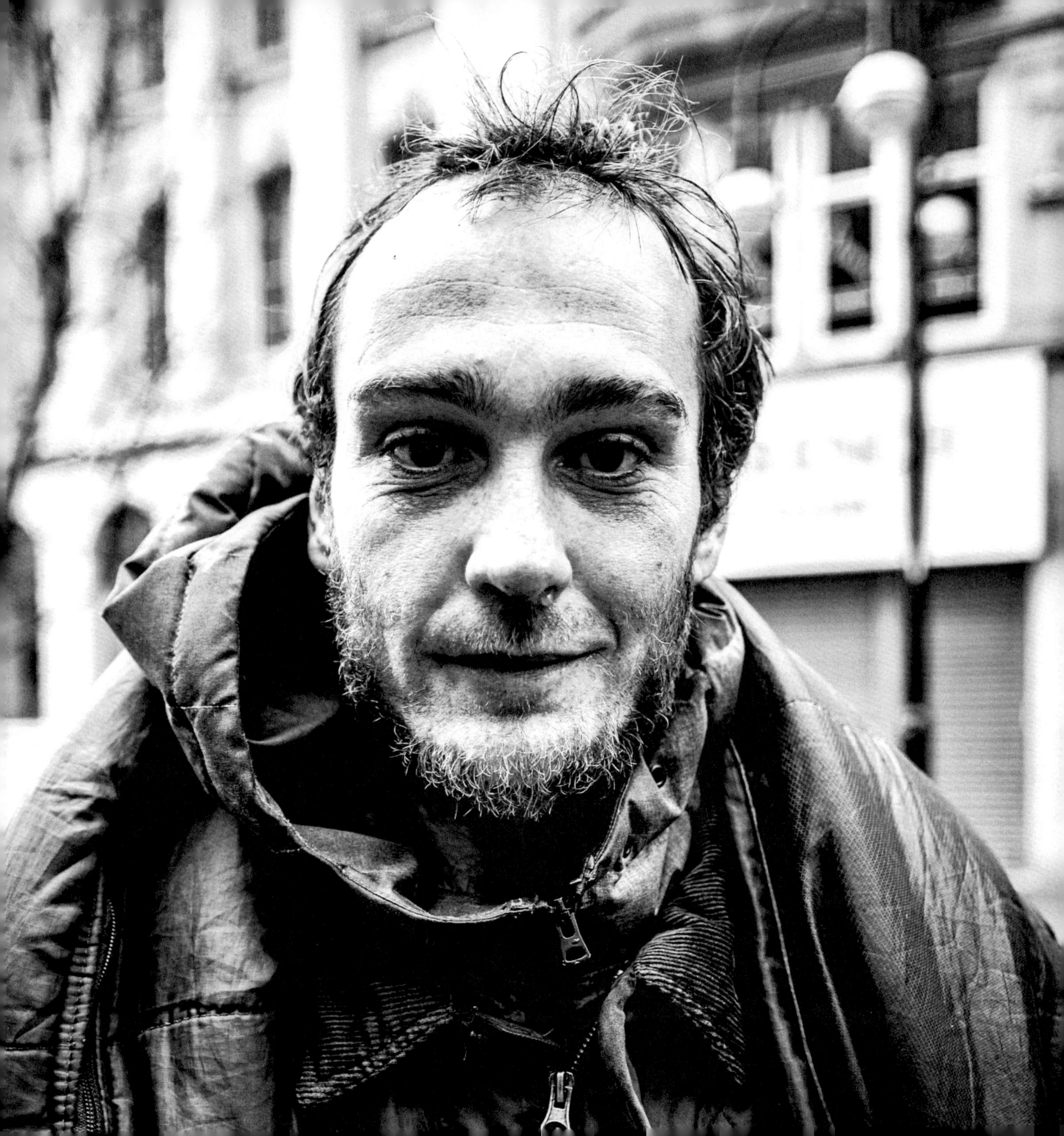

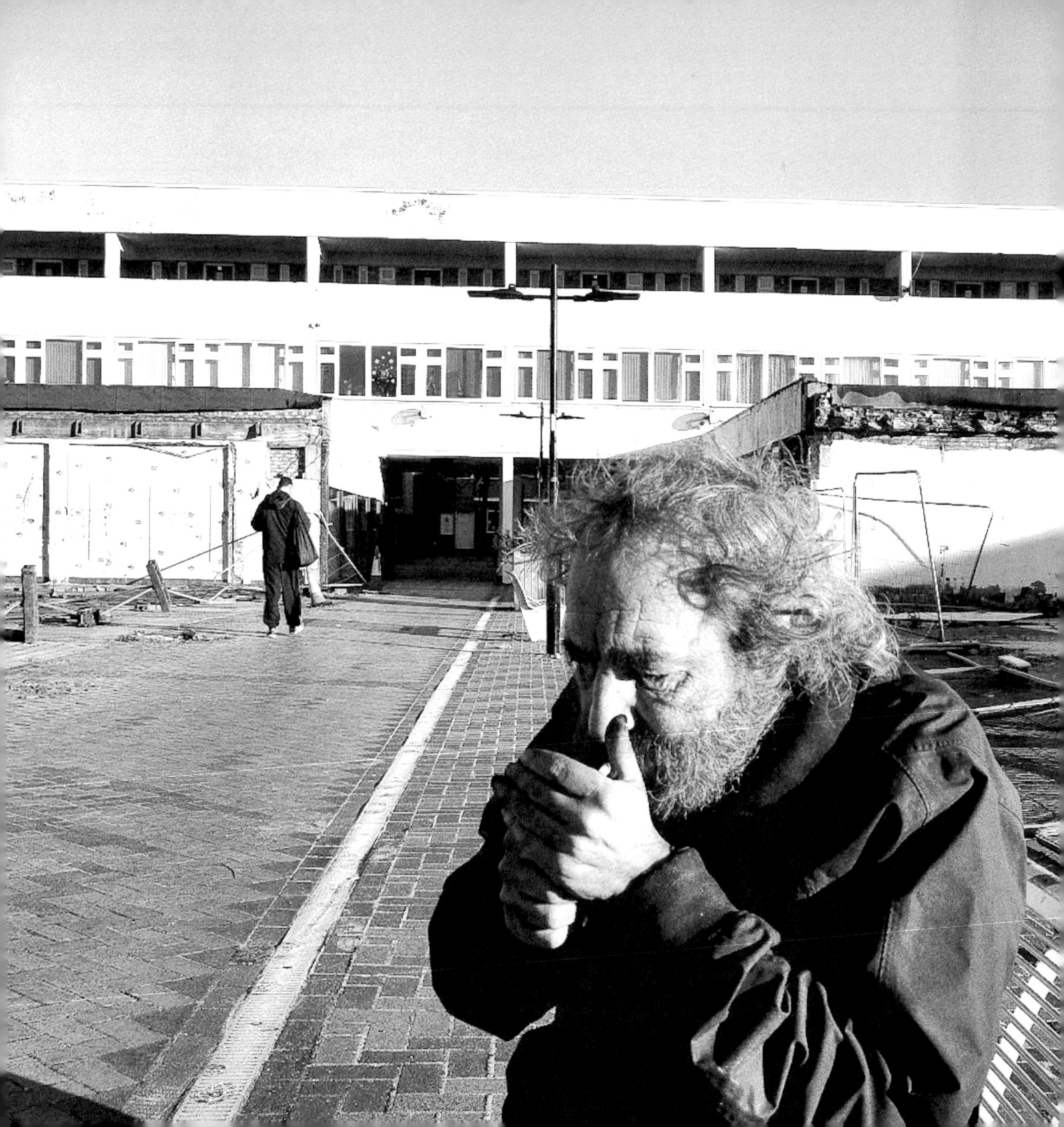

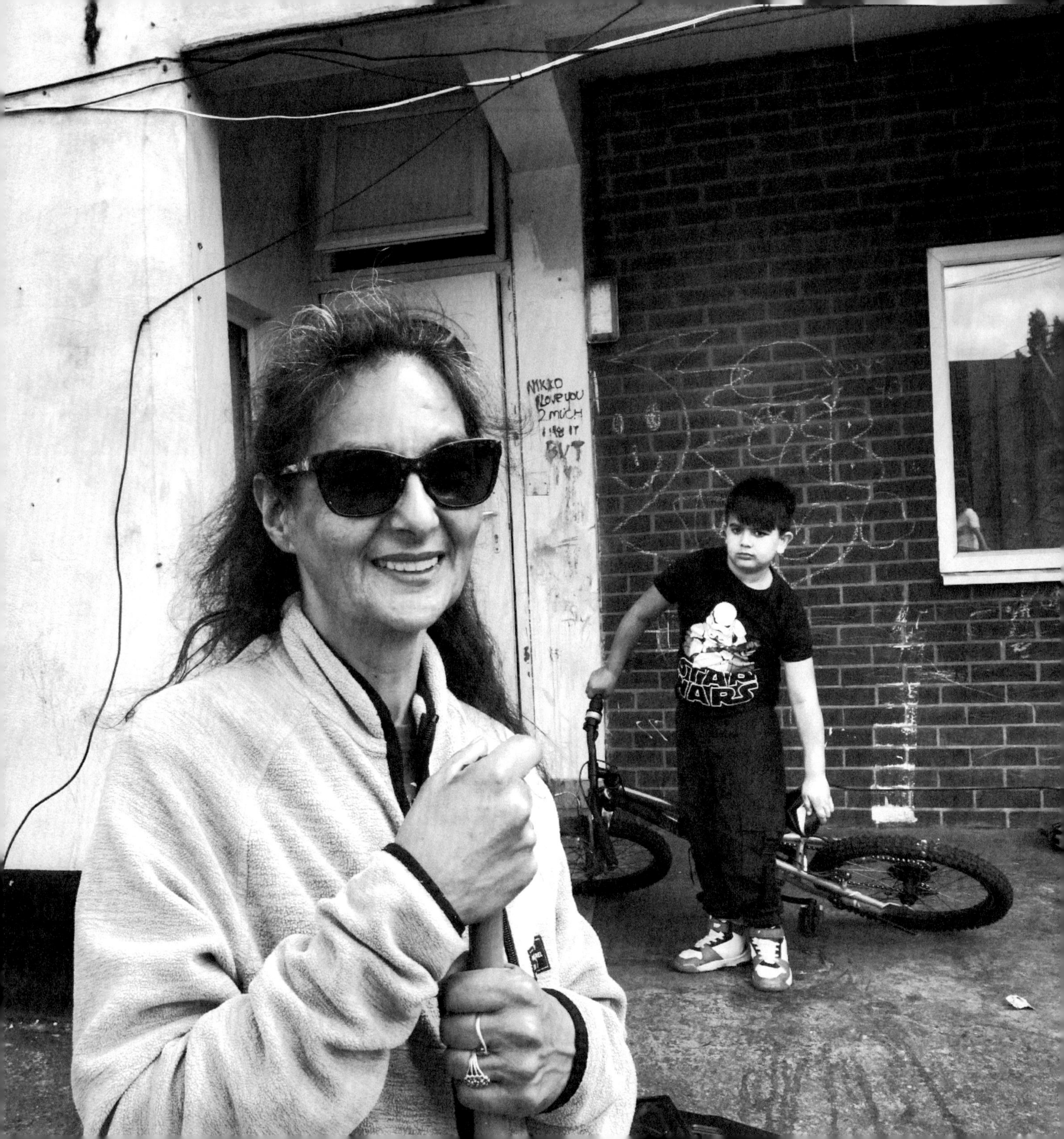

NIKKO
I LOVE YOU
2 MUCH
I H8 IT
BVT
STAR
WARS

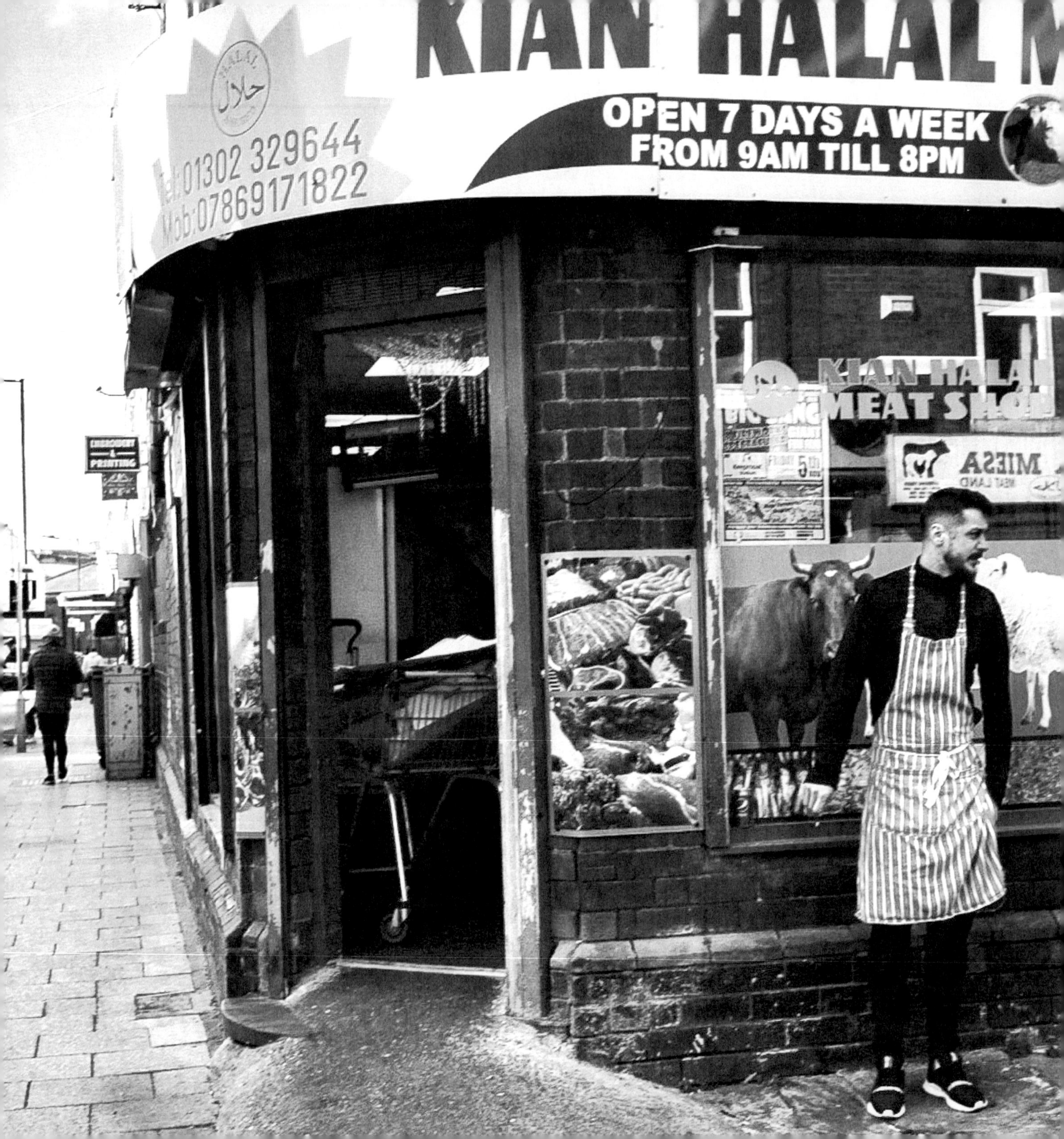

KIAN HALAL M
OPEN 7 DAYS A WEEK
FROM 9AM TILL 8PM
Tel: 01302 329644
Mob:07869171822
HALAL
حلال
KIAN-HALAL
MEAT SHOP
MIESA
MEAT LAND
EMBROIDERY
&
PRINTING